Peter H. Engel

The Dial Press
1976
New York

THE OVER-ACHIE-VERS

Acknowledgments

Lines from "Fifth Philosopher's Song" by Aldous Huxley:
Reprinted from *Leda* by Aldous Huxley (Harper & Row, 1920).
Used by permission of Harper & Row, Publishers, Inc., Mrs.
Laura Huxley and Chatto & Windus.

Lines from "What I expected, was" by Stephen Spender:
Reprinted from *Collected Poems* 1928–1953 by Stephen
Spender by permission of Random House, Inc. and Faber and
Faber Ltd.

Manufactured in the United States of America

First printing

Library of Congress Cataloging in Publication Data

Engel, Peter H
 The overachievers.

 Includes index.
 1. Executives—United States. 2. Businessmen—
United States. 3. Success. I. Title.
HF5500.3.U54E53   658.4   75-37882
ISBN 0-8037-6596-7

To my parents and to Samantha
I am deeply grateful

Contents

Preface

The other night I was a reluctant participant at a gathering of rather frantic East Coast liberals—the kind who insist that "organic" food is the only cure for a cold and that vitamins (of the meaning and chemistry of which they are entirely ignorant) are second only to clean air for enhancing virility. Those who, above all, insist (as they grace their swimming pools sipping their "in" rosé and comparing the hand-crafting techniques of their fifty-dollar shifts) that America is going rapidly to hell primarily because of its mercenary, "thing"-oriented outlook. I could not get away and so, like many a good-behavior prisoner before me, I tried to keep quiet and avoid controversy. I tried, that is, until an especially shrill female informed me categorically that all business was evil.

"We are being dominated by big business," she insisted, "dominated and dictated to."

Her husband, poor man, a well-paid actuary employed by one of our largest insurance companies, the funds of which alone support more industries than exist in many an underdeveloped nation, cringed. She had gone too far for him—and much too far for me.

"Are you dominated by your automobile?" I asked. "Or is it the heating in your house that threatens you?"

"My car pollutes," she argued.

"Can't you buy a bicycle?"

"I could. But no one else will."

"Then it is really your fear of what others will say or think that dominates you, not your car."

"I have a bicycle . . ." she said defiantly.

"Presumably made out of steel smelted with coal under conditions of what you would call 'pollution'; and by machines of huge power and energy consumption," I said. "A bicycle sold to you in a retail store which exists only because trucks roll and airplanes fly—eating air and gasoline."

She tried to interrupt, but I went on. "Your bicycle has tires, I imagine, as do most bicycles. They needed giant vulcanization plants for their manufacture. You ride over asphalt roads, which could have been built only by a highly industrialized nation." She was silent. "Do you truly feel dominated by industry?" I demanded. "Or do you revel, as I do, in the luxuries which are ours primarily because industry is strong and healthy?"

The lady fled to a less demanding conversationalist, yet I had said far too little. I should have tried to make her realize just how extraordinary is the strength and development of our society; I should have reminded her of the health and wealth of our people; I should have challenged her to walk down one of the incredible canyons of civilization—New York's Park Avenue, for example—and marvel at what man, and particularly *businessman,* hath wrought. There can be no doubt that the peoples of the industrialized nations are infinitely better off than those who live in nations lacking industry. When we call poor nations underdeveloped, we mean that they are *economically* underdeveloped.

Economic strength largely depends on the strength of business. There are countries with enormous mineral and agricultural wealth, such as Colombia or many nations in Africa, where most of the population is desperately poor because industry cannot exploit these resources; and there are other countries that have few resources, such as Japan, where industrial strength has permitted a large population to live in reasonable affluence. Literacy, higher education, health protection (from infant survival to a secure old age), and virtually every other aspect of comfortable living is possible only in economies that can afford and wish to pay for them. And they can only do so if business is sufficiently vigorous. Even health and longevity, considered over whole populations, show a fairly close correlation with the economic strength of those populations. The short work week, early retirement with pay, generous vacations, and above all, full or nearly full employment, are possible only when business is vital and growing.

Who buys the product that allows for the good life if not the employee of business? How many people could read Thoreau if his books were not printed by business, the inks for them not manufactured by business, the trees not harvested and pulped and pressed into paper for them by business? A paper mill worth probably a half-billion dollars is needed to make the kind of paper on which we can read Thoreau's hymn to simplicity!

Among all the industrial nations America seems to me to be by far the greatest and the best. Part of this is statistically provable, but statistics are often debatable. I speak of a feeling that goes far beyond statistics. There is an integrity to life in America and a concentration on ethics and values. Perhaps America's politicians *are* more venal than those of, say, England. Certainly America has a greater crime rate than Switzerland. But the American people fight for improvements and castigate themselves for shortcomings. They *care* to a degree rare in other countries—and the things they care about improve America and the quality of their lives. It is a luxury for an industrial society to reduce air pollution, yet in New York there is a steady annual reduction. It is a luxury to walk on the moon or to forecast the weather by satellite. It is a luxury to transplant hearts, to implement no-fault divorce laws, to vacation overseas, to work a short week, or to travel in "homes on wheels." But all of these are almost taken for granted by millions of Americans.

Since our early history, pioneering and achievement have

been an American trademark and a heritage. It was the need for freedom and land which drove the Pilgrims to America and the search for farm land that populated the Midwest. It was the gold rush that opened California and the railroads that fed and strengthened the entire country. The coal mines and steel mills of Pennsylvania made that state rich and the automobile industry built Detroit. The textile industry originally brought real wealth to New England (and it is no coincidence that much of the area suffered when this industry was largely destroyed by less expensive Japanese imports), and the oil-and-fuel industry gave Texas its enormous wealth. The list is endless. Industry, business—and businessmen—built the United States and developed its almost unimaginable riches.

The combination of a young, pioneering people plus great natural resources has made America into a country that has the largest, strongest, healthiest, and most dynamic industry in the world. Indeed, if the corporation sales were measured against the gross national products of nations, some *forty* American companies would count among the one hundred richest "nations" of the world.

Business health *is* the health of the economy; the health of the economy *is* the health of the people. Only by building industry, increasing wealth, and raising the standard of living can we overcome the problems which still plague the United States and, in far greater measure, the rest of the world. Pollution control is not a matter of will or technology; it is solely a matter of money. If we can afford clean air and water, we can have it.

But industry cannot prosper without dynamic, determined, successful leadership of the kind that cannot be supplied by the ordinary run of men. In my view only certain men and women in each company innovate, create action, and move things. The achievements of business are possible because the men and women in business achieve and, in some rare cases, over-achieve. The overachievers, whom this book seeks to find, define, and describe, are the essential fuel that drives all business. This rare person, whom I describe as the overachiever, may not be working for the good of the world. He may or may not believe in the old axiom that what is good for General Motors is good for the country—he may not care. He may, in some cases, be a "tainted saint" indeed. Adam Smith wrote in *The Wealth of Nations* that "It is not from benevolence of the butcher, the brewer, or the baker that we expect our dinner, but from their regard to their own interest." But I suspect that there is tremendous practical determination among businessmen today to do more than make profits. In any case, as a practical doer of good, as a veritable creator of progress, as a savior of the poor, the illiterate, and the ill, the businessman is nonpareil.

This book is a personal examination of the overachiever in business—my personal, pragmatic, opinionated outlook, my own maverick view, based not on psychological research or controlled clinical experimentation, but on the drives and experiences of my friends and my acquaintances. Grounded not in theory but in my close observation of their behavior and of my own, it is my opinion of what makes the overachiever run, how he runs, and even why. The new fad word (lifted from the anthropologists, who use it to describe behavior patterns and behavior influences in animals) is "ethology," so I might say that this book includes my views on the ethology of the overachiever.

I will be successful, however, just as businessmen are, only if I achieve some finite result with this book. I hope it will enable the reader to recognize those driven men who feel the need for change more than they feel the need for the safety of the *status quo;* I hope it will persuade him that the overachiever is an absolute necessity to business and that he must be searched for and encouraged and rewarded; I hope that it may help him, in a practical way, to know how to challenge and, in the nonpejorative sense, exploit those men in his organization who are capable of real achievement; I hope that it may assist him in recognizing how large and important a part is taken by certain overachieving men in business. Finally, I would hope that it will expand the reader's desire to make or encourage improvements, and to create action.

The Overachievers— What Sort of People

The best business organizations, like the most powerful rockets, are capable of reaching the moon, and can be made ready to challenge the stars beyond. The worst of them, like the Penn–Central Corporation, career to an inevitable crash. But neither a business nor a rocket can move off its launching pad by one inch—nor deviate by one degree from its course once it is launched—without some motive force, without that controlled explosion of energy we call its fuel. In industry this fuel is supplied by a certain special type of man or woman. He may be a president or a chief executive officer, or he may be found at the junior levels. It is this special person who creates action where there was none. Imperceptibly at first, the company or department stirs under his or her influence; then, apparently miraculously motivated, blasts off to achievement.

About ten years ago a little Brooklyn food company was teetering on the edge of bankruptcy. Its products were good, its sales organization was strong, but consumers knew little about its brands and the company could not possibly afford enough advertising to popularize them.

Somewhere in a back room sat a very young man earning the grand sum of

$325 a month. He was trying hard to cultivate a mustache in order to look older. His title was "media manager," but his job consisted merely of making sure that the right commercials got to the right television stations at the right time—such few commercials as the company could manage at all. It was hardly an exalted position from which to save the company, yet save it he did. Sitting there in his little back room, he created on his own several new television shows, developed the ideas, researched the facts, and wrote the words, learning the techniques of scripting and presentation from a TV-producer friend. When he was finished, he had some remarkable new programs ready for production. Still without informing management, he sold the shows for a combination of cash, which he needed to get them produced, plus a considerable amount of free television time, which he needed to advertise his company's products.

Today, that food company, many times the size it was, is very profitable—and is run by a tough-minded $150,000-a-year ex-media man!

The type of person who provides the fuel for industry is of peculiar and rare talent. Often he faces tremendous opposition or is forced to overcome immense inertia. Sometimes he destroys his health—although he is a healthy and hyper-energetic fellow, as a rule. Typically, he works like a dog and loves it. Usually he is gifted with humor; and always with sound intelligence. Importantly, too, he is a person who, with Thoreau, "hears a different drummer," and has the courage to "step to the music which he hears."

He is a logical thinker in business and, like all good business people, has trained himself to consider the available facts before he makes a decision, but his own behavior may exceed logic. His iconoclastic dissatisfaction with static institutions, his gut-tearing need to improve things, to get things moving, cannot easily be explained. Sometimes such a determined drive for improvement, such a scorn for the "path of least resistance," almost seems to transcend the entirely rational. It stems from some inner need which allows him to achieve more than other people who may appear to be as knowledgeable or as bright. Such men (and throughout this book I shall use "men" to include women because it is customary and less awkward) I call the "overachievers." They are the obverse of those designated "underachievers," those who achieve less, according to their ability, than they should. The underachiever is the well-known educational phenomenon, defined by the Department of Health, Education and Welfare as a person "with superior ability . . . whose performance . . . is significantly below his measured or demonstrated aptitudes or potential for academic achievement." In no instance is such underachievement explicable by major physical illness or serious psychological upset. It is simply the description of people who don't do as well as they should. How many of us used to receive report cards from school which said something like, "could do better if he tried"? That is underachievement—although it remains to be seen whether it is underachievement by the child or the teacher!

I had a friend in college, a brilliant, handsome, athletic man, a leader who was loved by men and women alike. We all used to congregate in his room and listen to him expound on everything from philosophy to football. He was a sort of college Socrates and we his disciples. He had a sonorous voice and, as I remember one of his girl friends remarking, the whitest-blond hair she had ever seen. And yet, the poor man became so nervous about his final examinations that he could never even sit for them. Although he led his class throughout the year, he nevertheless flunked out of universities in three countries. As far as I know, he never did get a degree. He was a pathological underachiever. I should add, as a sidelight, that in other ways his accomplishments were real enough. For example, he tutored his dedicated but rather dense roommate with rare patience, coached him endlessly, compensating vicariously for his own inability to achieve, until against all odds the roommate finally graduated from medical school. Some doctor! Some achievement!

The elusive spirit which drives the overachiever is not physically explicable. I believe it is inborn or developed very early in life. Thereafter, it can—and should—be fostered and nurtured, but I doubt whether it can be created where it does not, to some extent, exist. It is a virtue or a vice (depending upon your point of view) with which a man starts out or which he acquires early in life. Some men have a talent for song and others for solitude. Some men paint, others write poetry. Still others play tennis with uncanny skill. So, I believe, some men are endowed with a talent for "getting things done" and with an inner urge to spend their lives at it. These men are the movers and doers in whatever field they find themselves.

At first glance there appears to be no behavioral, physical, educational, national, age, or sex standard for the over-achiever. The men who move businesses come from an almost infinite variety of backgrounds. They create movement in many different directions. They are of varying degrees of intelligence. Their appearance may vary from strong and handsome to hunchbacked—although they are never lacking in vigor and drive. Their personalities may vary from ebullient to introverted. Certainly, their methods of achievement are infinite in variety.

One of the most extraordinary of the overachievers is Edwin Land, who created a major business empire on the basis of one fundamental idea which, so he claims, he developed in virtually all of its ramifications during the course of a single day. The fortune of his Polaroid Corporation, today a half-billion dollar company, has rested from its very beginning, as it does today, on inventions. The latest business advance of Polaroid is the development of a totally new camera and a totally new developing process which allows the film to develop a picture outside the camera and in front of your eyes.

Where Edwin Land build an empire and changed the picture-taking habits of the world through his invention, George Romney saved his empire, American Motors—and, at least in the context of the energy crisis which is today such an important concern, improved the transportation of a nation by popularizing the smaller car—through pure evangelical salesmanship. The "gas-guzzling monsters of Detroit" were the constant subject of Romney's taunts, as was the ridiculous sight of one ninety-eight pound housewife driving one forty-pound child to kindergarten in a five-ton automobile. Romney's achievement was great. It is instructive, therefore, to note that as Secretary of Housing and Urban Development, he never matched the fervor he possessed as president of American Motors, nor did he match the success. Perhaps he had reached his maximum potential as president of American Motors. As we will see in Chapter 11, even the greatest of overachievers may reach their limits.

Just as surely as George Romney saved American Motors, so Alfred Sloan saved General Motors. He did it, however, by an achievement which, while as great, was totally different. As chief executive officer of General Motors for twenty-three years, and a member of its Board and a participant on its Committees for forty-five years, he created what may be the largest and finest administrative organization the world has ever seen. In his book, *My Years with General Motors,* Mr. Sloan writes, with justified but understated pride, that for General Motors, which "at the close of the year 1920 . . . faced simultaneously an economic slump on the outside and a management crisis on the inside," it was his own "organization study" that "served the purpose." And yet, although Alfred Sloan was a genius of administration, that is not the most impressive thing about his book. The really surprising thing is that, in the midst of talking about his new organization study, and throughout the book as he describes the major ameliorations in administrative technique that emerged from his brain, his real and constant emphasis is on implementation, *on getting things done.* "The divisions naturally resisted this move . . . but I persuaded them," he writes of one idea. And again, "This memorandum was not a mere expression of regret for lost time but a preamble to a new program. . . ." And yet again, "General Motors is a growth company, and the sum of all I have said is expressed in this fact."

And finally, in the last sentence of the book: "The work of creating goes on."

Yet there is some similarity among overachievers, something alike in their psychological make-up, something in common— and, while it is hard to describe, it is as obvious as light to the naked eye. While it is true that a firefly is nothing like a fluorescent light and that neither is similar to the moon, yet all glow and in that one respect they are very similar indeed. Overachievers "glow" in many different ways, but always to a degree which so far exceeds the glow of ordinary men "as great'st does least."

Success comes, in major measure, to those who are overachievers. Some men have talent to such great degree that, even without the hunger for success, they cannot fail but attain some modicum of it. An amusing example of this is the story of a brilliant young man who wanted to "drop out" as a youth. But success dogged his footsteps.

As a youth straight out of college this young man became a salesman for a plastic sheeting company, apparently falling into the situation without caring much one way or the other, as a result of some contacts provided by his father. Nevertheless, within only two or three years, he had parlayed his job from simple salesman to ownership of a substantial sales franchise company representing one of the billion-dollar plastics concerns. He had sales offices and salesmen all over the United States and was well on his way to becoming a millionaire. He gave it away, however, impetuously and uncaringly, to his estranged wife. And, happy to be rid of his success (and I assume his wife), started again as the janitor of an apartment building. As he explained, it left him leisure to read.

To his chagrin, he was quickly promoted to building manager—with no time to read!

"I had no alternative, as I saw it, but to quit," he said.

When the money he had saved while reading and managing was gone, he went to work for Macy's as a stock clerk.

"Surely, I thought, I could sleep behind the pallets," he said.

Again he failed; for within days he was promoted to sales clerk. Soon, unable to sleep behind any pallet—and bored to tears with standing behind the counter —he decided, for amusement, to put on his own private sales drive. For three consecutive weeks he was the most successful clerk, in sales, in the Macy's chain. Inevitably he was promoted to junior buyer, no closer to his ambition of dropping out.

Determined, though, as this young man is, he again quit his job and this time joined an advertising agency as a mail boy.

"If they wouldn't let me sleep," he explained, "at least I could run around in the open air with never a care or worry."

Unfortunately, within two weeks he had made a suggestion on a piece of advertising which he happened to see.

"I should have bitten my tongue off," he said.

And so he was elevated again, this time to copywriter. And then, within less than a year, to account executive and finally, meteorically, to account supervisor.

"They sent me to Harvard to study how to be the success I desperately didn't want to be!" he explained. "So I decided, after all, to espouse ambition and welcome the success-destiny which constantly was thrust upon me."

Once he had made that decision he went to the opposite extreme and started working toward success with zeal. He achieved enormous feats, but his enthusiasm lasted only a year or so and finally his drive for underachievement got the better of him. He left to go back to university as an undergraduate in a field he had never studied. "Surely there," he said, "I should be able to find a way to do practically nothing."

The last I heard of him he had become an assistant professor whose classes were crowded to capacity.

What similarities are there among the great innovators, the great movers, the great achievers, and how can these characteristics, once defined, be nurtured and expanded? The answers to these questions are the subject of this book. The inner, psychological similarities among overachievers can, of course, be expressed in a variety of ways. A great deal of work on this subject has been done by psychologists who seek to measure the "need to achieve" or the "motive for success" (called N–Ach and MS respectively), but the subject is worth briefly investigating here. What are the similarities between overachievers which can be observed during the normal business day?

The most fundamental explanation of the overachiever stems from the idea of the drive to dominance, observable in man as in a thousand species. It is obviously true, and virtually universal, that in the societies of insects, birds, reptiles, and mammals there is a clear and important ranking, a well-established pecking order. In a chapter entitled "Who Pecks Whom," Robert Ardrey, in *African Genesis,* the first of his fascinating, "popular" books on anthropology and ethology, writes: "Every organized animal society has its system of dominance. Whether it be a school of fish or a flock of birds, or a herd of grazing wildebeest, there exists within that society some kind of status order in which individuals are ranked. It is an order founded on fear. Each individual knows all those whom he must fear and defer to, and all those who must defer to him. Self-awareness in the limited sense of consciousness of rank seems to have appeared at some very early moment in the evolution of living things."

But the point is not that such dominance is inborn (although its potential may be), but rather, as Ardrey points out, the dominance "is competitively determined fairly early in the individual's lifetime." Nor, as Ardrey and others emphasize, is it solely dependent on actual physical superiority: much of the dominance in the animal kingdom is by voice and bluff and not by tooth and claw. The dominant male, even though he is unlikely to be the weakest, need certainly not be the strongest. He is merely thought to be so—by others and by himself. That would appear to be the key: overachievers are those who are so aware of their own abilities and strengths that they thereby convince others that they are truly superior. As a result, they enjoy the ability to lead; they can achieve more than their actual degree of superiority really warrants.

The question remains, however, whether it is achievement itself that teaches the dominant individual to trust in his own strengths; or whether he is blessed in the first place with a sense of superiority which allows him to achieve. Like so many intellectual conundrums, this is one that, on the one hand, would seem absolutely to demand an answer, but on the other is as hard to resolve as the proverbial question of whether the egg preceded the chicken or vice versa.

Jane Van Lawick–Goodall spent many years observing chimpanzees at the Gombé Research Center near Lake Tanganyika in Tanzania. She describes her observations graphically in her book, *In the Shadow of Man.* I believe that what she observed suggests strongly that dominance is the *result* of achievement, not the other way around. I am convinced that chimpanzees develop dominance by *learning that they can achieve.* In the case of chimpanzees, it is hunger which drives them to achieve; later, it is the experience of achievement which leads them to the assumption, by themselves and by their peers, that they *are* dominant.

By a giant leap of conviction—admittedly no more than hinted at by the observations of the anthropologists—I move from chimpanzee to man and suggest that it is achievement which also creates dominance in the human. It is an almost circular argument: achievement creates a feeling of dominance and that feeling fosters achievement. *Almost* circular, but not quite. For the original ability to achieve would still seem to be inborn, or at least inculcated at a very early age. So we see that the argument turns out to be not circular after all. Even better, it is also rather optimistic. It suggests that even though the innate talent for overachievement cannot be created where it is absent, it can be greatly nurtured where it exists. It is possible to enhance enormously the ability of the overachiever by making it possible for him initially to accomplish some achievement. The confidence that this first faltering step will bring may be sufficient to loose a torrent of further achievement—which in turn may lead to such self-confidence that the achiever may perform to his utmost limits—and perhaps well beyond his apparent ability. Making available to the young businessman the opportunity for achievement is perhaps the most important and fundamental skill business must learn if it is to train and develop the overachievers it so urgently needs. How it may do this is a key question that I shall discuss later.

A second and different view of the overachiever lies in Ralph Waldo Emerson's thought that the way "to do is to be." The man who achieves *is,* and in Emerson's terms "he exists in a crowd for himself and lives the way he thinks, not caring how others think of him." Emerson's essay on self-reliance is one of the most illuminating on the subject of the overachiever. It clearly shows that achievement need not be something based on extraordinary talent but rather something based on extraordinary desire to state things as one sees them, to develop one's own thoughts and then to turn them into actions or attitudes of one's own. "To believe your own thought, to believe that what is true for you in your private heart is true for all men—that is genius," Emerson writes. "In every work of genius we recognize our own rejected thoughts; they come back to us with a certain alienated majesty," he continues. It is this "recognition of self" or self-reliance which appears to be another major aspect of the overachieving personality.

It is self-reliance, too, I suspect, which comes out in yet another form in the overachiever: the willingness, indeed the desire, to accept responsibility. It is an unusual and valuable man who is not only prepared to accept responsibility but who is truly at home with it. It is the man who, seated in the committee of which he may be merely a junior member, is seen to listen very carefully to what is said and then synthesize a solution to the problems being discussed, surprising all the others by actually telling them what should be done. I am constantly amazed by how difficult it is for many men to make decisions. Not infrequently business trains a man so well to see the alternatives— and to recognize the danger of choosing the wrong one—that instead of teaching him to make the best decision it inadvertently inhibits him from making any decisions at all.

The problem gets worse for such men as they progress, for the decisions become graver and the responsibility of making the wrong ones heavier. There was a chief executive officer of a $75 million European company so mired in his growing inability to make any sort of decision that there came the day when, quite literally, he was unable to decide in which of four rather comparable restaurants he would entertain some business guests. Trying to persuade him to choose one over the other was one of the more agonizing of my moments in business.

The ability to make decisions without agony and to accept easily the responsibility for them, right or wrong, is one of the defining characteristics of the overachiever. He is rather existentialist in his outlook, less prone to what William Barrett in his book *Irrational Man* has called the "divorce of mind from life." He views his contribution as "real" and is therefore far less neurotic about his thoughts as contradistinguished from his actions. Either he creates action from what he thinks—or else those thoughts are of little importance to him. Indeed, at the risk of some overstatement, it may simply be that he finds the rather bitter pill of self-recognition a little less unpalatable than do most men. For him the fear of Zarathustra, who says "I was afraid of my own thoughts, and afterthoughts," is less telling. The acknowledgment of "the heaviest and blackest in himself" is not so overwhelming. For he deals not with the profound Nietzschean questions of philosophy and madness but with simple and precise acts measurable in hard terms for their achievement quotient. He either made it or he didn't; if he didn't there must be a reason, and a way to achieve a success the next time.

These psychological identification marks and the palpable quality of leadership innate in the overachiever, together with a healthy—and, I suppose, occasionally unhealthy—dose of rampant ambition differentiates beyond question the overachiever from the rest of humanity.

Alvin Toffler has written about the "future shock" of too rapid change. The overachievers, I believe, experience the opposite. They suffer from "past shock": an inability to exist without positive change, without making at least an attempt at improvement. It may be they, with their need for improvement and their scorn for the *status quo,* who are the most responsible for the Toffler-stated dilemma that common man cannot keep up with the changes created by the leaders of men—although I must add that I do not believe Toffler's dilemma exists, at least not in the way that he suggests it does. I doubt whether even the most dynamic innovator can move the population more rapidly than it is willing to move. I believe that, not infrequently, overachievers (especially while they are still young and too impatient) fail to survive within a particular company because they cannot move the organization forward as quickly as they want; and the less improvement the company shows, the more concerned they become until finally they can stand it no more and, facing up to the inevitable, they move on. *These are the men who are traumatized by the improvable.*

The overachiever is probably more open to creative thought than other people, although he is not necessarily more "creative" himself (as we shall discuss later), and that is one of the clues to his success. Indeed, as Arthur Koestler writes of great inventors in science, his characteristics may include "The belittling of logic and deductive reasoning (except for verification after the fact); horror of the one-track mind; distrust of too much consistency." The point may be exaggerated, but nevertheless it is useful in order to throw some light on the type of healthy impatience the overachiever always exhibits.

Another characteristic of the overachiever is that he has a great desire to please himself, to do what he wants to do. "We are all of us compelled to read for profit, party for contacts, lunch for contracts, bowl for unity, drive for mileage, gamble for charity, go out for the evening for the greater glory of the municipality, and stay home for the weekend to rebuild the house," critic Walter Kerr has written. But the motivator of industry differs from Mr. Kerr in that those are precisely the things he *wants* to do. Mr. Kerr may be compelled, muttering acerbic cynicisms, to read for profit; but there are undoubtedly those who devour the dullest prose and thrive on all those other tasks as well, crying for more, in their enthusiasm to achieve.

Finally, overachievement is frequently tied to necessity, frequently personally inspired inner necessity to be sure, but for the fueler of business, real necessity nevertheless. A man driven by some inner instinct for achievement is very like Eric Hoffer's "adventurers and outcasts," of whom he wrote in *An American Odyssey:* "If in the end they shouldered enormous tasks . . . and accomplished the impossible, it was because they had to . . . and once they tasted the joy of achievement, they craved for more." Indeed, "craving" may be the most important, or at least the most *operative* word of all. In business it may very simply be that people who don't crave don't achieve. "In a time of pestilence," wrote Camus, ". . . there are more things to admire in men then to despise." That is, of course, because necessity is not only the mother of invention, but also without doubt the father of achievement!

If anyone doubts the importance of *necessity* in creating a desire for action, let him consider the amazing surge of creativity *and* implementation that came over the people of England during the Second World War when the entire nation was fighting for its life. Men, who in their civilian lives had contentedly pushed paper from pile to pile, suddenly implemented fantastically complicated and fantastically efficient administrative systems for rationing food; for civil defense; for the production necessary for the "war effort"; for national health; and for a myriad of other programs dictated by necessity. Men who had been entirely satisfied to sit back behind little shop counters suddenly, on their own initiative, led desperate attacks across the front lines into the face of the enemy's fire —and won! Men who had been content to fish in the waters of the English Channel as their forebears had, suddenly and spontaneously organized themselves into a civilian "armada" and rescued the British Army at Dunkirk. Here was innovation and implementation of an incredible order carried out by men who in more normal circumstances had been neither creative nor action-oriented.

Necessity turns most men into overachievers. We are evolutionarily programed to survive and it is therefore an evolutionary inevitability that we should meet real necessity with real achievement. But if our heritage requires us to fight for survival when disaster looms, then it must, too, teach us to sit back and relax when things are going well and there seems little to strive against. With no challenge, most men would see little need for great achievement. It is the man who feels a challenge all the time, even when others feel none—and when, seen objectively, there is none—who becomes an all-the-time overachiever.

Marshall McLuhan seems convinced that overachievers are merely a figment of their times: "Mighty corporation chiefs of Bismarckian quality and Teddy Roosevelt enthusiasm become standard properties of every well-managed enterprise," he writes in *Take Today: The Executive as Dropout.* But he is wrong. Facile, but wrong in the sense that, again and again, organizations flounder because no true overachiever emerges—or the *wrong* one does.

Where is the great Borgward automobile company which, in its heyday under Borgward the genius mechanic, created some of the most exciting engineering breakthroughs in the modern automobile? Where do the great railroad barons, who colonized the West and industrialized America, slumber? Whatever happened to Botany suits or Lofts candy or the Packard (and almost to the Rolls Royce) or to a myriad of other firms who made decent, sometimes excellent products at a fair price? They went out of business or into various forms of bankruptcy and either ceased to exist entirely or, at best, continued to eke out a limited and unhealthy existence waiting, quite probably in vain, for the day that a new overachiever, a man like the one who built them to greatness in the first place, would emerge to take their helms and lead them back to glory.

Some railroad companies have metamorphosed into successful and growing corporations; many candy companies are profitable; and surely the automobile industry thrives. The failures I have mentioned and a vast number like them (Mr. McLuhan notwithstanding) are memorials to the fact that, without the right man, no company can be successful; and memorials too to the equally certain fact that no guarantee exists that the right man, the man with the right degree of drive for overachievement, will be found at the time he is needed.

Fortunately, the right man frequently does emerge. It will be found that, in high degree, he has the inner qualities I have mentioned, i.e., the drive to dominance, inborn but augmented by the experience of success; self-reliance, or as our offspring describe it, the willingness to "do your own thing"; the ability to make decisions without agony (because he views them as pragmatic); an almost neurotic need to improve things; a nontraumatic attitude toward facts; an openness to new thinking, often mislabeled "creativity"; the enjoyment of what he has to do to achieve; and the feeling of necessity for action, whether it stems from real or imagined challenge. As we shall later discuss, these qualities are transformed in the business world into observable characteristics in men who are potential overachievers.

Beyond the personal, inner make-up of the overachiever, he is also differentiated by his style of living and his attitude toward life. Certainly, he travels more than other men.

Phil Beekman, the incredibly determined and hard-working president of Colgate–Palmolive, International, in the year he first took over responsibility for Colgate's Latin American and Caribbean business, traveled so much that, *including* holidays, weekends, and Christmas, he was able to spend only eleven days at home.

One man, working for a small candy company, was able to prove the advantages of travel when he landed a major contract for his company simply because he responded to a blind telephone call from Dallas. He arrived in the ninety-degree Texas sun firmly clutching his briefcase and in winter clothes at ten the next morning. His far stronger rivals over at the Hershey Company were still writing memoranda to try and decide whether it was worthwhile to pay the expenses of a junior executive's trip to Dallas.

I should hasten to add, however, that traveling, per se, does not indicate achievement, but it is, in many instances, necessary for rapid achievement. There is of course a small class of people that travels professionally, constantly, all around the world, carrying passports as fat as dictionaries. Some are the expert advisors and others the supervisors of far-flung multinational corporations. Airplanes and hotels are their dwellings, movement their *status quo*. Among them, in the same proportion as among other groups of businessmen, there are to be found overachievers as well as ordinary men. The amount of traveling they do provides little clue to which.

The overachiever has more entertaining friends; he is more curious, more aware. Stuart Shaw, a tight, hard-driving little man who was, at one time, a middle manager in good standing at the Procter and Gamble Company—although a maverick, which quality led him later to join *Playboy* and move from there to a whole variety of other entertainments—invented a concept to compete with and be more useful than the well-known Intelligence Quotient or I.Q. ratings. He called it A.Q., or Awareness Quotient. It is not a measure of how intelligent a man is, but rather of how wide awake and "with it" he is. While the concept was originally developed as a party game through which Stu would measure participants' A.Q.s by asking clever and funny questions drawn from current events, it has some usefulness. A knowledge of what is happening, an openness to the changing world, an acceptance of new ideas, all these are signs of the overachiever. It is safe to say that, as a rule, O.A.s have high A.Q.s.

I think it is fair, too, to say that the overachiever lives harder. He works longer hours, wastes less time, reads more, views less television (unless he is a television expert—in which case of course, he views more television and, miraculously, manages to remain sane in spite of it), and generally lives life to its fullest. He has the energy and the drive and he burns it freely to have room for more. Energy, in this respect at least, is like love: the greater the amount used, the greater the amount available. The overachiever sleeps better, *when* he sleeps, because he sleeps from healthy tiredness, not from overweight boredom. Indeed, there is a fair degree of evidence that the overachiever is, on average, substantially healthier than is the run of normal men.

Dr. A.T.W. Simeons, in his book, *Man's Presumptuous Brain,* explains that whenever there are causes for "panic" in modern man (by which he means worries or tensions), even if these remain below the level of consciousness, there are immediate physiological reactions. If there is no release for these reactions —and what sedate businessman can afford to flee screaming through the streets every time sales decline—then "the perfectly normal diencephalic responses begin to pile up, and sooner or later the worker will suffer from such psychosomatic diseases as high blood pressure, diabetes, chronic diarrhea, or a coronary thrombosis." The overachiever, however, is less fearful and is therefore far less apt to develop the desire to flee and therefore less likely to experience the physical symptoms of frustrated flight. Rather, self-assured, certain in his ability to achieve, he undertakes the tasks necessary rather than worrying about whether he can handle them or not.

Another way of looking at this aspect of the overachiever stems from the work done by Neal Miller in the 1950s and early 1960s in which he proved beyond a reasonable doubt that rats, at any rate, can be taught to control their heart rate, blood pressure, and so on. Indeed, by 1969, Miller was able to insist that psychologists should think of the actions of the glands and internal organs of the body in about the same way as we normally think of muscles. In other words, Miller has finally brought some scientific evidence to what the yogi has known all along. Indeed, in a flabbergasting experiment conducted in 1970 in New Delhi, Ramamand Yogi demonstrated, while he spent six

hours or so in an airtight box, that he could, by will and medita-
tion alone, live on approximately half the theoretical minimum
level of oxygen needed for human survival. For significant portions of the experiment, Ramamand Yogi was able to live on
about a quarter of what Western science believed to be the
minimum.

The point of this obviously is not that the overachiever is a
man of yogi-like qualities, but rather that there is a strong
suggestion that will power alone—and the overachiever obviously has an abundance thereof—may be sufficient to affect the
so-called involuntary functions of the body and thus positively
affect health. I have no doubt from pragmatic and personal
observation that men of great energy and great achievement are
thoroughly healthy. In spite of what, on the face of it, would
appear to be tension-filled lives, they are frequently the most
relaxed and well-composed of men.

The overachiever is, at least in later life, generally more pros-
perous because he is more successful, and he enjoys the ac-
couterments of prosperity—big homes, comfortable cars, smart
restaurants, fine clubs, exotic vacations (for which, however, he
rarely takes the time) all form some part of his life. It is interesting to note that, typically, he is not liable to Veblen's "conspicu-
ous consumption," for just as he is interested in action and not
words, so he seeks fun rather than the appearance of fun and,
more rapidly than other men, he will discard tinsel. The really
opulent house, the garish sports car, the excessively modish
dress tend to be the hallmarks of the overachiever's son! Certainly, he takes advantage of his wealth, but rarely does he
flaunt it. He has the self-confidence of achievement and does
not need the added boost of parading his "net worth" in front
of the world.

In many ways the family of the overachiever gains tremendous
advantages, both economically and psychically, from its associ-
ation with him. He stimulates, excites, drives, encourages, enter-
tains and most effectively supports. But his family has major
problems too, for the overachiever is away a great deal of the
time, comes home late, is terribly busy, relocates frequently,

inadvertently demands a great deal, and then demands more. His are not the degrading demands of a slave driver, but rather those of a brilliant professor. Bright children and a bright spouse in an overachiever's family can have a wonderful life; but a dull or slow child or a "girl next door" wife who never grew would probably be crushed. In the family, the normal pressures and reactions of the business world apply, only with greater intensity.

Finally, the overachiever probably lives longer, not only because, as noted, he is more capable of controlling his life through determination and action but, I suspect, because he thinks of death as the ultimate underachievement!

The Face of
the Overachiever:
How to Recognize It

The task of finding, recognizing and hiring the overachiever is the most important thing that a businessman can do. In business, as in the world, "man is the measure of all things," and it follows that only great men can achieve greatly. Recognizing overachieving characteristics in current employees or in candidates remains by far the most difficult of the businessman's tasks. Many men are knowledgeable and competent and have good track records on paper. When you ask their previous employers about them you rarely get anything but a favorable report.

The drive to get things done; the urge to compete; ambition; determination; dynamism: these are the qualities you are looking for. In fact, however, they are all facets of one overriding characteristic of the overachiever, a characteristic that can best be summed up in one word: "hunger."

Harold Geneen, President, Chief Executive Officer, guiding genius and absolute leader of ITT, one of the largest and most successful conglomerates in the world, is certainly a candidate for the title of the hungriest man alive today. He has been enormously successful both for his corporation and personally and one might wonder why he aspires to greater wealth or power. Yet he continues to work ceaselessly to amass more of both. He has established a system of controls in ITT which demands performance from every department and every manager—and if a manager does not perform up to his standards there is no excuse: Geneen is reputed to work sixteen to twenty hours every day and to be completely and undeviatingly dedicated to success.

Norton Simon, the great collector of art and companies, with a reputed fortune of over $100 million, has said of himself that he is a driven man: "Some people are born with peace of mind, I am not. In the Dostoevskian sense, I am a suffering man. . . ."

W. Clement Stone would undoubtedly echo that sentiment. Three times as rich as Simon, and probably the most successful salesman the world has ever known, he would probably express the idea in words more suitable to his salesman's attitude of positive thinking. But, "play to win" would be just as much his motto as Simon's. Indeed, the series of early-morning chants which many sales companies now use to arouse and excite salesmen are almost his invention. They are his way of packaging his own drive, his hunger, for the benefit of more phlegmatic men.

The very rich "are different from you and me," wrote F. Scott Fitzgerald. Had he been talking about those members of the very rich who are also self-made, he could have added, "because they are infinitely hungrier."

At the other end of the spectrum is my good friend Dick Pinkham, Senior Vice President of Media and Programing for the Ted Bates advertising agency. He is an intelligent, urbane, and delightful man, and moreover, has a capacity for achievement which only very few are capable of matching. The *Today Show* was not only his (and Pat Weaver's) idea, but he organized and brought it to reality. When it was not going well, he developed the incredibly crazy idea of putting a chimpanzee into the middle of this serious news program—and for many years J. Fred Muggs was the leavening which made the serious parts of the *Today Show* more palatable and thus gathered for it an enormous audience. It was Dick Pinkham, too, who conceived the original idea for the nighttime talk shows, and under his leadership the *Tonight Show* became a success. Moreover, those achievements, which have affected the education and communication habits of an entire nation, are only two of a wide variety of other achievements. As a result of who he is and of his record, Dick has been offered the presidency of at least one of the major television networks and of at least two huge advertising agencies. I know of few people who would be more capable of running such organizations.

But Dick Pinkham prefers to continue where he is, and to savor fully his present good life. Certainly he works hard at his job, at public television, and at a substantial number of charitable duties; but he is so good at what he does that he has plenty of time left over to enjoy himself sailing, or playing golf, on cruises, or at home with his family. He is content with his major and influential position in the communications world and does not aspire to that pinnacle of power that is found only at the presidency of a major company. Dick is a major achiever—but not, by his own choice, an *over*achiever in the world of business.

The difference between Harold Geneen, Norton Simon, Clement Stone and their ilk on the one hand and Dick Pinkham on the other is neither in ability nor in creativity. Certainly, it is not in intelligence or in judgment. It is simply that the overachievers are a tremendously hungry lot. Men like Dick Pinkham are marvelously genial and generally satisfied with the way things are.

The inevitable question is, of course, whether for the hungry man his hunger is a good thing. Is he benefited or harmed? In the case of the Geneens, *et al.,* the hunger seems a blessing. On the other hand, its absence is patently not a problem in Dick Pinkham's case. Perhaps the point is hardly worth considering, for the fact is that one doesn't really have a choice. It seems to me that one either has this unappeasable need to get things done —and then more and more things—or one does not. All that is certain is that without this often illogical need for forward motion, without this arational but insatiable urge to get ever more things completed, without the inner motivations that drive certain men but leave others in peace, there is no such thing as an overachiever.

The world of psychology has developed a battery of personality tests that are thought to be useful by many psychiatrists, psychologists, and counselors. They include the complicated (and often ridiculed) Rorschach, the Minnesota Multiphasic Personality Inventory, the Bender–Gestalt, to name just a few. If they are effective in helping psychologists understand their patients, then it would seem that they could be equally useful in helping to recognize the overachieving personality. Unfortunately, many psychologists—most notably the behaviorists at the University of New York at Stony Brook on Long Island—feel that the tests are of "little validity and less value," as one of them put it. Moreover, even though a great deal of work has been done by behavioral scientists in translating these and other diagnostic tests into practical interviewing techniques, most businessmen continue to feel that they are not practical in their daily work. In sum, they feel that psychological testing can be discarded as a practical tool.

Nevertheless, some way of recognizing the potential overachiever is possible; a description of him can be made with reasonable accuracy. Once he is clearly described, he is far easier to recognize. Thus, with the caveat that no definition of the overachiever can be wholly accurate, I suggest that there are, in order of importance, nine observable attributes which together make up the truly successful overachiever.

The first I have already talked about. It is simply hunger. But it would be a mistake to assume that all hungry men succeed. The psychological traits which can be summarized as hunger are indeed a requirement for overachievement, but there must be a lot more. The question, then, is what are the special characteristics which convert the successful man *into* the overachiever? Or what other qualities does the hungry man need in order to be able to use his hunger effectively? The balance of this list should answer that question.

The second attribute is intelligence, an elusive quality in itself. For one thing, it is difficult to measure. I.Q. tests are no sure guide. Most of us know what we mean by intelligence, at least as it is needed in the workaday world of business. And intelligence is the quality which is able to cover almost every other weakness, except, of course, the lack of hunger. Indeed, intelligence can sometimes be the antithesis of hunger since it may add too much logic and common sense to that state. "Why should I be so hungry?" the intelligent man may ask. "I have all I need." Since hunger is, after all, an "irrational" drive, excess intelligence may be a *neutralizing* force. *It is a very sly asset.*

The third requirement is energy, the purely physical force necessary to carry out the desires created by that key requirement, hunger. Good health is, generally speaking, part of this requirement of energy—a man who is unhealthy is not likely to have the energy needed for real achievement. But health need not entail complete "wholeness." Franklin D. Roosevelt, a man unable to walk, had boundless energy. Real weakness, however (a heart that can stand no stress, or constant pain), are clearly incompatible with great achievement.

The fourth attribute is tact. The greatest problem any overachiever faces is in moving men and organizations he is likely to cause disruption. The less tactful and the more abrasive and disruptive he is personally, the less likely he is to achieve his ends. It is often hard to persuade a group of men inculcated with one procedure that another is better; it may be impossible, if one is also personally disliked. Change is not always easy, nor is it always gratefully accepted. Taking this into account, the wise businessman takes great care always to tread softly, and with tact.

The fifth characteristic is persuasiveness or salesmanship. It is a quality born out of hunger by intelligence. The persuasive man is driven by his hunger to convince others; and by virtue of his intelligence is usually able to put that drive into words. While it is not a universal truth, it is a pretty good rule of thumb that intelligence is closely related to the mastery of language.

The sixth essential quality is humor. There is a danger among men of great hunger that they may drive each other, or themselves, crazy. Humor is as necessary in the hungry man as is lubrication in a racing engine. As Arthur Koestler pointed out, "the luxury reflexes of laughter and weeping emerged as overflow mechanisms for the disposal of at least part of our redundant emotions."

The seventh attribute is courage. The overachiever's life is full of risk. The unknown, which he seeks to explore, is magnified for him; it tends to be a frightening place. The overachiever requires the courage to shed his old skin and risk the new, tender skin underneath in an unknown world. In this respect he is very much like a growing caterpillar. The underachiever, on the other hand, having an overwhelming fear of exposing himself, never sheds his old skin, never risks damaging the new—as a result, he is quite unable to grow, quite unable to change his lowly state.

The eighth quality is optimism. Men have only a limited amount of courage available and it is quickly dissipated if every possible danger of the unknown is not only fully explored and considered, but also fully felt. Optimism of the type I mean here is that state of mind which allows a man to *adjudge* a situation realistically, but then to *feel* that things will turn out well. In these terms Charles Dickens's Mr. Micawber was no optimist but a poor fool, and his constantly reiterated hope that something would "turn up" merely a fool's hope. On the other hand, the overachiever's *knowledge* that he is making a decision which has a 75 percent chance of being correct, tempered with a *feeling* of confidence about his decision, is business optimism of the right order. It is a necessary asset for, without it, courage would have to be excessive.

The ninth and final requirement is creativity. This comes last on my list not because I hold creativity in low regard but rather because a first-class man of hunger, intelligence, energy, tact, persuasiveness, humor, courage, and optimism can surely recognize a good and productive idea when he sees one. Even if he cannot generate great ideas himself, he can buy them from others who have a talent for creative thought but are not themselves movers and doers.

However, this quality of creativity is one of the most complicated to define so that, depending on the definition, it may turn out to be the single most important of all of the qualities, save that of hunger, after all. If what we mean by creativity is the ability to develop ideas, then it is, as I have said, a desirable but not an essential asset; but if we mean the ability to think differently from others, then it seems to me that creativity is, indeed, as Toynbee said, "a matter of life and death for any society" and, I would add, for any business. Arthur Koestler, in his superb book, *The Act of Creation,* explains creativity as an act of "bisociation," i.e., the act of combining two unconnected facts or ideas into one new idea. For example, if you take a detergent and combine it with dirty clothes in a wash to get clean clothes, you do not have an act of bisociation since you are combining the detergent with something else, dirty clothes, with which it is associated by its very nature. But if you take the same detergent and put it into the water at the base of a cut Christmas tree in order to lower the surface tension of the water and allow more of it to be absorbed into the tree, thus preserving it longer, then you have two unrelated items, the detergent and the Christmas tree, being "bisociated" into an idea. Talent in bisociation is, of course, desirable in all men. But if it leads to ideas and only ideas as its result then it is of limited advantage because nothing concrete happens; since it is not a particularly rare talent, it can be readily purchased. On the other hand, if it leads to the idea as the *starting point* to implementation or problem solution, then it is a talent given to few—and those few are the overachievers.

Perhaps we are simply playing with words. For the fact of the matter is that creativity defined as the ability to find and implement new solutions for the "impossible" is probably very closely related to what I have called hunger. E. Paul Torrance has written at length about creativity, and I don't propose to repeat very many of his words here. But I think that I can summarize that part of his thesis which is germane to my point in a short sentence or two. Writing of the creative individual in a book called *Guiding Creative Talent,* he says that a talented individual is "fully alive and open to awareness of his own experiences and those of others and seeks to organize them and see meaning in them"; and that he "has a need to prove his personal worth and dramatize and display his ideas"; and finally, and most tellingly, that he "enjoys intense, sustained, and vigorous effort to surmount obstacles." That, of course, is what *I* call a hungry overachiever! Hunger in sufficient measure may inevitably result in creativity.

The knack for the facile idea, the easy notion, is not achievement. It may exist in the underachiever and be conspicuously absent in the overachiever. It may be *called* creativity, but in a fuller sense creativity may be said to carry with it the implication of great determination to get the problem solved—and great courage. "Society in general is downright savage toward creative thinkers," says Torrance. And Emerson before him lamented that "society everywhere is in conspiracy against the manhood of every one of its members." If not to the same degree, at least to some extent, business is also hard on the manhood of its overachievers. Only a man with the qualities of courage and humor in great abundance can hope to survive in any human community, including the business world. But this is especially true if he is gifted (or cursed) with the dual capacity to bisociate and thus create new ideas, *and* to implement the ideas created. This type of creativity, as distinct from that type which is purely generative of ideas, is more than one of the important attributes in men who overachieve: it is the very hallmark and essence of the overachiever.

The one quality that appears to be missing from the list of nine characteristics which together seem to me to be the vital attributes in the man who is to achieve the extraordinary is a quality dear to the heart of most personnel men the world over: it is "the ability to get on well with people." Obviously it is akin to tact, but it is not tact alone. Indeed, I have known men of considerable tact who could not get on well with people at all: they bored their friends half to death! This ability is omitted here not because it is an undesirable asset—indeed it is an absolutely essential one—but because *tact combined with the ability to create action is the ability to "get on with people."*

J. Paul Getty, Howard Hughes, Harold Geneen and other men of enormous achievement have not necessarily been likable. Sometimes they have succeeded in spite of a lack of tact—although most are more tactful in fact than they are in reputation. But they have been tremendously liked, almost revered by those close to them. Alfred Sloan and General MacArthur were, at best, cool and standoffish men in their workaday world. But again, men would have laid down their lives for the first and readily did so for the second. Churchill drove people crazy— but he was loved by a nation. Senior executives of excellent caliber, men who move mountains, achievers in high places or low are usually loved. But even if they are *not* loved, they are always in the end admired and often revered for their abilities.

All of this leads to the general observation that overachievers usually end up with large and loyal followings. Often this is because such men have, in superabundance, supplies of tact and charm—enough at least to compensate for those occasions when their excessive drive becomes abrasive. More often, these men command loyalty because they introduce action and movement to lives, and corporations, which have been starved for both. The result is a mood of excitement, of action, and since most men cannot create action themselves, they follow with devotion those who can. The widespread exodus from a large company that usually follows the resignation of a controversial corporate monarch is only partly because his employees were loyal to him—or tarred with his brush. Mostly, they leave because life without his guiding light becomes plain dull.

After all these careful definitions, we are left still squarely facing two questions: "How do we find the overachiever and persuade him to visit our company for an interview?" and "How do we pick him out of the crowd of interviewees—assuming he is in it?"

The basic answer to the first question is that if an overachiever is looking for a job in a company with a particular set of business circumstances, he will come looking in any company which reveals those circumstances. To oversimplify, it is only necessary to show the right "face" to have the overachiever bang at your door; it must be a true face for the overachiever will sooner or later discover the false one and either not join or leave. The sort of face which attracts the overachiever will be discussed in detail in Chapter 12. For the moment, however, let it suffice that attracting the overachiever is a passive, not an active role. He will find *you*, knowing you for what you are, and come after the job. Now it is up to you to encourage him to take what you have to offer.

The second question, then, how to pick him out of the crowd once he does visit your office, is more actionable. How can we correctly select the overachieving man during the typical period of one or two job interviews which may last no longer than an hour each? How should we conduct the interview? What sort of tests should we administer? What should we look for in the interview situation?

Most men who regularly interview many job applicants develop their own interviewing techniques. Some are, of course, whimsical; others serious and carefully thought out and prepared. But all, if they are to be successful in recognizing the overachiever, must seek to determine whether or not the applicant has the right quality of hunger.

An interviewing technique one middle manager loved to use to differentiate the determined from the timid was to say to the applicant: "Sell me something." It often worked and he continued to use it for over a year—until one day it backfired dramatically:

"Sell me something," said the manager. And then, noticing a copy of *Life* magazine lying on his desk, he added: "Sell me a subscription to *Life.*"

The young interviewee started making a thoroughly professional sales pitch. It lasted a few minutes, and the manager was delighted.

". . . and so would you prefer a three-year subscription or a five-year subscription?" the young man ended.

"Excellent! Very well presented."

"Well, which is it to be, a three-year or a five-year subscription?"

"Okay, you did a good job," said the manager.

"Well thank you, but I have an order form here. It just so happens that I'm working my way through college selling subscriptions to magazines and I really would like to know whether you'd prefer a three-year subscription or a five-year subscription."

He paused; and the manager paused. But the young man continued first. "I assume that a man of your caliber would prefer a five-year subscription. I'd appreciate your signing this form that I've made out."

The interviewing manager was unable to get rid of the young man, by threats or by laughter, until he had bought a five-year subscription to *Life* magazine! But along with the subscription to *Life,* at least he knew that he had on his hands a remarkable young driver, a man of real hunger, a man likely to attain unique achievement.

Eric Morgan, now president of British–American Tobacco's cosmetic businesses, and one of the more brilliant evaluators of men's drives and hungers, used to ask applicants quite casually how many uses they could think of for an ordinary bottle. The answer, of course, required an exercise in imagination which was a useful piece of information for Eric to have; but, in addition, since he often made the request in a social setting, it gave him an excellent opportunity to evaluate a man's competitive instincts, his will to win in even the most relaxed of circumstances.

Another interviewing technique is to ask sudden and totally irrelevant questions. For example, the interviewer might ask, in the middle of a description of the applicant's business background: "If you were stranded on a desert island, what three men would you like to have with you?" I once asked my two sons, then twelve and ten, that question.

The older boy answered, pragmatist that he is, with a choice of three stalwart and useful people of his acquaintance: one to handle the cooking and exploration of the island; one to build an airplane to escape; and a third to keep the four of them entertained by his humor. It was a full answer which most of us would support.

But the younger boy, who is nothing if not a creative thinker, instantly had a totally different answer.

"I would take a Puerto Rican, a Black, and a Chinese," he said.

"Why?" I asked.

"So that we could all start equal," said the ten-year old.

There are, of course, also many formal methods which companies use to try to recognize the potential overachiever.

One major consumer-goods company, which has a reputation for picking the best men, used to give all its "successful" young men a test consisting of an arbitrary set of questions. They would then ask new applicants the same questions with the presumption that any new man whose pattern of answers was similar to the "success norm" would enjoy similar success. There was, however, little attempt to relate the content of the test to the reasons for success.

On the face of it, the test made sense. If an applicant exhibited the same pattern as the successful people within the company then, logically, he would be equally successful. Unfortunately, it was, in fact, a hopeless tool for picking out the overachiever from the crowd: the crowd, even the successful crowd, are the followers, not the leaders of men. To pick out the leader, the overachiever, requires a technique capable of differentiating him from the mass, not of aligning him with it. As a result, this tool failed completely as a predictive method for finding the overachiever, and was eventually dropped.

There is one technique for interviewing which is rarely used, but which is effective in differentiating between a potential overachiever and a successful administrator. The technique is incredibly simple: *ask the man!* Ask him what he views as his main strengths. Few men will falsely claim hunger and a drive toward achievement as key strengths if they do not have them. Indeed, in their absence, they will probably not even think to mention "achievement" as one of their strengths. Only a man with truly Chinese dexterity at Ping-Pong will consider the game worth mentioning when asked about special skills! On the other hand, overachievers are very likely to answer in terms of achievement because that is how they think. Moreover, as a sort of bonus, I have found that overachievers are rather precise about all their other strengths and weaknesses when asked about them.

Generally speaking, the more achievement-oriented a man is, the more objective he will be about his capabilities and his shortcomings; if he has few of the latter he will, of course, be unable to spend much time answering questions about them. On the other hand, in a more profound sense, he will find it easier to assess and define his own weaknesses, even if he has few, because overachievers measure their abilities by achievement —just as does the interviewer. And achievement—or lack thereof—is a very clear and objective fact. The characters in Jean-Paul Sartre's *No Exit* are underachievers, both in fact and because they cannot see or admit to their own poor level of achievement. I suggest that you simply ask the interviewee when you can think of no other technique; while you will not get a complete answer, you will be delighted, I think, at the truthful and useful responses you *do* elicit.

Even though there are some techniques which will tend to pinpoint the overachiever, none is definitive. As I said before, a great deal more work should be done in the area. So far, however, neither competent interviews nor the tests given by great companies are sufficient. Then how does one with certainty recognize the overachievers? What *measurable* qualities do they have?

The answer lies in actual, not stated achievement. If the overachiever in business is born—or born and developed—not bred, it follows that his drives have been with him, to some significant and measurable degree, all his life. Ask most men the question: "What have you *done* that is out of the ordinary?" and you will be met with a blank stare. But, just occasionally, you will find a man who tells you . . . and tells you . . . and tells you!

One of the most dramatic examples was the case of Mike, a meek, fair-haired boy who came shyly into the interviewer's office one day and sat perched on the edge of his chair, knuckles clasped white, and apparently wholly anxiety-ridden. "What extraordinary experience or idea have you participated in?" the interviewer started, probably feeling thoroughly pessimistic.

Mike shifted uncomfortably. The first syllables out of his mouth were in a high-pitched voice which seemed not quite under control, like that of an adolescent whose voice is breaking. But what he said—and it turned out to be absolutely true—was overwhelming.

"Well, I founded a paper mill in a Central African Republic. Then I sold it to their Government and came back here to complete my Masters Degree. And now, you see, sir, I am out looking for a job with a good company like yours . . ." He paused, and then in a strong, manly voice he added: "A company truly interested in *action.*" And his fist slammed the table, making the paperweight—and the interviewer—jump.

Joe, who is today a successful entrepreneur in Montreal, described a similar experience in which he was the interviewee. He was asked by the rather pompous personnel officer of the major Canadian corporation to whom he was applying for a job shortly before graduation, "What have you *done?"*

"I studied for my undergraduate degree and my CPA degree concurrently," he said. And then, while the interviewer nodded in appreciation, he added: "And I tutored other students in economics; and worked as the full-time comptroller of the Royal Victoria Hospital in Montreal." Of course, the interviewer was surprised.

Another young man looking for work after college, was asked whether he had earned any of his college tuition money.

"Yes, I did," he said.

"What sort of job did you have?" The interviewer looked skeptical because the young man was only twenty and looked less.

"I had several jobs."

"So tell me, tell me."

"Well, I sold roofs, door-to-door," he started.

"What else?" the interviewer interrupted.

The young man decided to drop his diffidence. "I organized the university typing pool; published notes for chemistry courses; translated sales material from German into English in Munich; looked for tetrafurfurylsalicylic acid in France; worked as a garage mechanic in England; organized a door-to-door sales force selling mops; chauffeured a car from Toronto to Vancouver; and worked in a cut-rate fur store," he said in a rush—and then added cheekily, "among other things!"

The interviewer immediately accused him of lying. When he proved that he was not, the interviewer hustled him out, full of apologies. Later the young man received a letter which today, as president and chief executive of a large cosmetic company, he still cherishes. It said: "We feel you are somewhat too energetic for this company."

It would, of course, be easy to find the overachiever during an interview if his achievements were always recognizable. Unfortunately, however, particularly in young men whose achievements are still somewhat limited by age, many achievements look smaller or greater than they really are.

A candidate for a management-trainee job was highly recommended by the personnel department because he had shown such initiative in traveling the world, but after talking for a while the interviewer was not impressed. No doubt the candidate had traveled the world, alone and with considerable initiative, but in all other respects he seemed to lack drive, to be somehow weak and undetermined. There was no other sign of his initiative. Indeed, it seemed amazing that he had been able to travel so broadly with so little apparent energy. The man giving the interview decided to probe further.

"What passport do you carry?" he asked.

"I have a Turkish one and an Italian one," the candidate answered. And then, apparently to make a better impression, he added, "My parents came from Chile. Actually, I was born in England."

The explanation was clear. He was no determined traveler. Traveling was, for him, the *status quo,* and no achievement. For this young man, staying in one place would have been a far more impressive achievement.

On the other hand, I had the experience of interviewing a twenty-seven-year-old man of considerable presence. He made an excellent impression, but when I probed I could find no outstanding achievements. He had worked for one large company as a salesman and then joined another in another part of the country as a district sales manager. Not bad, but pretty standard. Yet I sensed that, lurking somewhere below the surface, there was a great deal more. He exuded an inner power, an energy spark which should have shown through at some point in his life. But try as I could I could find no evidence to support my feeling as we talked of his business and his earlier college career.

"Are you married?" I asked, trying to steer the conversation in a new direction.

"Yes." I thought the answer perhaps a shade curt.

"Children?"

"Four."

"So many!" I said, surprised. "How does your wife manage?"

"Look, is this essential to the job?" asked the young man. "Frankly, I value the privacy of my home life."

It was a bold, almost rude statement, full of chip-on-the-shoulder defensiveness. I was amazed both because it had come practically with no warning and because he was not, in any other way, a defensive person. Obviously, while his family did not interest me per se, I had to find the reason for this strong reaction.

It took care and a good deal of time, but eventually I found the facts and with them I found the achievement. Apparently, his first wife bore twins and then, tragically, a deaf baby, whereupon she had a nervous breakdown and ultimately a permanent mental collapse. For the early years of his business life, he had not only worked but had also institutionalized his young wife, brought up two healthy babies, dealt with the tremendous difficulties of a young deaf boy, found himself a new wife willing to put up with all these difficulties—and a lovely woman she turned out to be when I met her later—and had a fine fourth child with her. In the context of all these problems, his apparently standard business achievements started to seem almost phenomenal. I hired him, of course, and he became one of the strongest young businessmen I have seen—a true overachiever.

Another reason that the overachiever may be difficult to recognize in an interview situation is that, especially in large companies, he has learned to keep his achievements quiet, to "internalize credit" in Harlan Cleveland's words. Indeed, in his book *The Future Executive* Cleveland goes so far as to suggest that achievement in the future, at least in large corporations, will be possible only by men who can perform silently and anonymously. While this is, in my view, overstating the case, I do agree that there is a most useful breed of executives, including overachieving ones, who operate by leaving the kudos to others and keeping the achievement as their own, inner satisfaction. Indeed, these men depend on the fact that they threaten no one and make no one jealous in order to get things done. No doubt Machiavelli achieved more than did his prince, Lorenzo the Magnificent, to whom *The Prince* is dedicated. No doubt, too, Machiavelli did not trot around boasting of this fact. Often it is difficult to pinpoint these men as action creators—or to differentiate them from other men who *boast* of achievements which they never influenced.

Indeed, ultimately, while there are many helpful partial answers, there is no complete answer to the question, "How do I recognize an overachiever during an interview?" Careful interviewing techniques are important in giving the overachiever the opportunity to present a true picture of himself. Of even greater help is probing and pushing to determine what the interviewee has already accomplished—and making sure that those accomplishments were real and not simply the result of following a predetermined "path of least resistance." But the fact remains that, as Peter Drucker writes in *The Effective Executive*, "People-decisions are time-consuming, for the simple reason that the Lord did not create people as 'resources' for organization."

One of the problems with selecting a suitable overachiever for business is that there is a tendency to try to pick "well-rounded" men who are competent in all respects and weak in none. This, I am convinced, reduces the likelihood of obtaining a real overachiever. There are few really strong people who have no partly offsetting weaknesses: the activist is often accused of being abrasive; the man driven to action is sometimes driven to rage; the man who is truly creative may, in some respects, be the biggest problem of all. He may lack practicality from time to time, or seriousness. He may even seem childish on decorous occasions. As Eric Hoffer puts it, "Both the revolutionary and the creative individual are perpetual juveniles. The revolutionary does not grow up because he cannot grow, while the creative individual cannot grow up because he keeps growing."

An overachiever may be a "generalist" or a "specialist" in his knowledge and training; whichever he is he will achieve more of what he attempts—and indeed he will attempt more—than will the ordinary man. But he need not necessarily be a man whose strengths are evenly distributed. Ordinary people, that is, those whose physiques conform to the average, don't become superstar athletes. But a man may become a fantastic footballer even if his arms are relatively weak—provided he has developed a marvelously strong torso and legs. It is typical of the overachiever that he has concentrated upon his strengths until they have overwhelmed his weaknesses and have become the essence of who he is. The question then is not whether a man has strengths and weaknesses, but rather whether his strengths are sufficient to get on with the job, to get things done. President Lincoln was told that his newly appointed commander-in-chief,

General Grant, had a drinking problem. He is reputed to have answered: "If I knew his brand, I'd send a barrel to some other generals." The point was that Lincoln knew that Grant, and not McClellan or any of his other unsuccessful generals, was the man to get things done, was the overachiever, with or without his weakness, who could win the war.

One thing that you can be sure of: if, by good judgment or just plain good luck, you have employed the right sort of over-achieving man in your organization, it will rapidly become obvious. Suddenly you will notice that the media department is not only turning out more and better analyses, but is buying better time; or that new market-research techniques are being tried and are giving better results; or that sales in your Venezuelan subsidiary are booming. And if you look (and are not yourself dyed in any corporate tradition of "we don't do things like that") you will find some young person working twenty-five hours a day and getting things done. You will then know that you were successful in recognizing an overachiever. Don't let him go to waste.

Overachievers
and the
Anatomy of Action

Plutarch wrote of the great orator Demosthenes that, when he was asked what were the three most important aspects of oratory, he answered "Action, Action, Action." Thomas Henry Huxley wrote that "The great end of life is not knowledge but action." And, some time near the end of the second century before Christ, Quintus Ennius exclaimed for the first time in recorded history, "No sooner said than done—so acts your man of worth."

Yet, while some men constantly create action others, who appear to be as competent and of as great "worth," do not. We have already discussed some of the reasons why certain men are so driven to action. But the question remains: how do they achieve it?

In examining the methods of achieving action we must first dispel two major myths: the first is that action is created only by vigorous, outgoing men and that quiet, introverted people never get anything done. We might call this the "Mike Todd Syndrome." The second myth is that thought is to some extent the antithesis of action. The corollary of this myth (if myths can have corollaries) is that men of great wisdom who bring to events a sense of historical perspective do not, as a rule, move current events as rapidly as do youthful firebrands. Notwithstanding Shakespeare's conviction that "action is eloquence," many of us continue to believe that men capable of writing or talking lucidly, let alone eloquently, are unable to turn their thoughts to deeds.

First let us deal with the "Mike Todd Syndrome." There is of course no doubt that men like Todd create action. Such men stand out in any field as the ultimate overachievers; they abound on the front pages of newspapers; they are scattered throughout business and indeed throughout every successful institution— and they are enormously effective. They are notable because they are newsworthy. *But* they are by no means the exclusive creators of action.

Moshe Dayan is an Israeli and a world-wide folk hero, complete with a buccaneer's eye patch, a face of almost cherubic innocence, and a string of scandalous liaisons with beautiful women. He marches across the pages of modern Middle-Eastern politics and war with all the swagger and dash of Errol Flynn at his best. General Bar Lev, first as commander-in-chief of the Israeli Army, then as minister of commerce and then, while still minister, as one of the three or four men who stepped in to rescue Israel when it was unprepared at the start of the Yom Kuppur war of 1974, has achieved just as much for Israel. He carries just as much power and will probably be written about in history books with just as much adulation. But Minister Bar Lev is a quiet, white-haired man who smokes a pipe and talks in soft, measured tones. Few would think him ebullient. None would think him ineffective.

The cosmetics business has typically attracted the most rambunctious of extroverts. Charles Revson, who founded and built the Revlon empire, Helena Rubinstein, Elizabeth Arden, Estée Lauder, and many others were all dramatic people with a flair for self-publicity, and outgoing, often domineering, frequently tyrannical personalities. Their companies achieved great success. But Yves Rocher, a quiet, shy, completely introverted man who grew up in a northern French village, founded the Yves Rocher Cosmetics Company. Started later than the others, it is already a substantial concern in France, and it is growing faster than many of its competitors.

I would guess that there are as many successful quiet men as there are noisy ones. Nevertheless, extroversion is frequently *thought* to be synonymous with action. I believe the reason is that the ebullient person frequently appears to be very open— open to ideas, solutions, attempts—whereas there are certain types of quietness which probably are incompatible with an open mind: the personality types that are closed of mouth because they are closed of heart. But I doubt whether there is much evidence in the psychologists' journals of any real correlation between open mouth and open mind or its converse. The extrovert may be appearing to agree, may be promising to act. But action, when it is actually measured, depends not on who talks about it most. Gertrude Stein wrote that "A rose is a rose is a rose is a rose" (thereby excluding all extraneous coincidence about flower gardens, assistant groundsmen, etc.) and, I suggest, he acts who acts who acts who acts! Certainly, if quietness is not a symptom of a closed mind then it need not be a symptom of an inability to achieve action.

The myth that action is inhibited by thought, the "Stuffy Professor Syndrome," is nonsense on the very face of it. If it were not, all human endeavor would be disastrous indeed, for all action would be essentially thoughtless. Only a cynic of really overwhelming bitterness would believe this. On the contrary, most of us would agree that thought is a vital precursor to action and, with John Locke, we would feel that "the actions of men [are] the best interpreters of their thoughts."

Bernard Baruch, one of the most successful financeers and speculators Wall Street has ever known, described how he used to withdraw for several days, just to think before taking one or another of the decisive actions that created his enormous fortune. During those times he was away from his otherwise hectic life and insulated from "action." But I think we are dealing merely with semantics, for there is action in the sense of achievement and action in the sense of mere activity. It was not from action but from activity that Mr. Baruch was shielded; action in the achievement sense is what he was creating. He was its very motive force. It was such quiet action and unhurried achievement which made him rich and allowed him to become a great philanthropist.

"Events are not rushing anywhere, we are merely consuming them at indigestible speed," Russell Baker wrote in one of his delightful columns in *The New York Times*. Sometimes wisdom appears to be the opposite of action simply because the wise do not rush to consume events at indigestible speed. In fact, there is nothing in the least antithetical between thought and action. Frequently, indeed, frenetic action, in the sense of activity rather than achievement, is a large stumbling block in the way of getting anything done.

The thesis of this chapter is that there are specific, systematically describable methods and techniques for creating action. It is my belief that these techniques do not correlate to any significant degree either with extroversion or with lack of thought. It is my further belief that they can be described, and even taught. In summary, the techniques of achieving action can be broken into the following six component parts.

1. The first step (underlining my view that thought is a necessary precursor to any successful action) is to do the thinking necessary to establish the problem. There is probably more time and effort wasted in the business world on administering events without defining problems then on any of the "great procrastinations" we shall discuss in Chapter 5.

"Declining sales will inevitably lead us into the red. That is our greatest problem," wrote one chief executive officer. Few of the recipients of this doomsday note disagreed. But the fact was that declining sales were not his problem at all, they were merely a symptom.

The reason for the declining sales of this particular company was that the company had no new products. There was no excitement; consumers generally felt that the company's products were good but dull. They were uninterested in buying. Detailed market research indicated that consumers answered the question: "Why don't you buy the company's products?" with one of several versions of the same basic answer: "What have they done for me lately?"

Further investigation showed that the lack of new products was still not the core problem, only a more clearly defined symptom. The reason that no new products were being developed by the company was that even though a great deal of effort was being made by some excellent men in both research and development and in marketing to develop exciting and effective new products, no one could ever agree as to which new product should have priority. This constant disagreement resulted in a "stop and start" situation: in the end, no new product was finalized.

At this point in the analysis of the problem it appeared that the constant disagreement among the middle-management executives was close to the "heart of the problem." Even so, it was still not the problem itself. The real problem in this case lay one step further away: it was that the chief executive officer, an eldest son who had the training but not the guts for the job, was unwilling or unable to decide which new product or products should have priority. Without his lead, the company was bound to flounder.

Eventually the company declined so far that its bankers thought it necessary to bring in a new chief executive officer. He quickly analyzed the "problem," chasing it back along all its limbs until he found its real heart. Simply, quietly, his pipe relaxed in his hand, he designated which items were to be the top-priority, new-development products. Within months, they were developed, marketed and the company sales started to climb again. "He is a man of action!" they said.

The first principle of action is to find the frequently elusive problem. There is a simple technique to doing this which can and must be practiced. Above all, the danger of assuming that a symptom is a problem must be avoided.

The method of chasing down the symptoms until the heart of the problem is discovered boils down to asking and then re-asking the simple question "why?" It is necessary to continue to ask that question until it is simplified right down to one clearly defined and easily understood problem, a problem so simple that action can immediately be implemented to eliminate it. This technique, which I call "The repetitive 'why?' " can be readily practiced. Here are some examples of its use:

a. A company's sales were growing faster than the industry average, but profits were declining, whereas industry profits were rising with sales. (As noted above, this type of general problem is almost always a symptom, not itself the heart of the problem.)
Why?
b. Because the company's cost of goods, as a percentage of sales, was rising. (If this had been taken to be the problem, then the management directive would have been "lower the cost of goods." But no one would have known how to do so. No action would have resulted.)
Why?
c. Because raw materials were rising in line with inflation while selling prices were not rising as fast; nor were they rising as fast as competitive prices. (The now obvious action would have been to raise prices. To be on the safe side, however, it is always worth asking "why?" one more time to see where it leads.)
Why?
d. Because the sales manager objected to any price rises on the grounds that raising prices would tend to slow sales growth.

Now the heart of the problem had been uncovered. In considering this answer it seemed obvious that rapid sales growth had become the objective of the company, regardless of profitability. There seemed no reason why the company's prices should not rise. The needed action was very simple and clear: persuade or, if necessary, order the sales manager to raise prices. This was done and, while unit sales growth did indeed slow slightly, dollar sales growth actually accelerated—and profits started to climb.

a. The sales manager of a medium-sized pharmaceutical company had the problem that retailers handling his merchandise complained of slow deliveries and generally bad service.

Why?

b. Because there was a constant shortage of inventory even though there were no raw material shortages, strikes, lack of factory capacity, or other obvious reasons for the shortages.

Why?

c. Because the forecasting system did not produce what the sales department sold. (If this answer had been accepted without further questions, the decision would have been to tell forecasting to do a better job—hardly a practical command since forecasting was already trying its best.)

Why?

d. Because the historical data fed into the computer by the forecasting department led to forecasts very different from the actual orders as they subsequently came in from customers via the sales department.

Why?

e. Because the company had a long history of poor shipments. Thus, what was actually shipped (and eventually reported to the computer as historical sales data) was not reflective of what customers wanted to buy. Rather, it was reflective of a combination of what customers had wanted and what the company had had available to ship.

Thus, the real problem was wrong computer input. The action was to ask the sales and the marketing departments to make a forecast of what they thought would sell rather than relying on a computerized projection—and then to ask the factory to produce according to that new forecast. The problem was largely solved. Eventually, as the forecasting technique became better and actual sales fell into line with what the trade wanted to purchase rather than what the factory had available, the computer input data became better and the computer forecasting system was reinstated. From that point on everything went smoothly.

a. A small company was on the verge of bankruptcy despite the fact that profits appeared to be reasonably satisfactory and sales seemed to be rising fast: the company was simply running out of money for working capital and was unable to borrow any more.

Why?

b. "Because those damn bankers refuse to lend us any more."

Why?

c. Because the liquid ratio was approaching dangerously close to 1:1. (If it fell below that, the company was likely to be in trouble. Most healthy companies have ratios well in excess of 2:1.)

Why?

d. Because the company frequently needed to borrow more than $100 when it made a $100 sale.

Why?

e. Because the sales department frequently took orders for items not in the company's line. In that case, in order to buy the packaging materials and product components at a good price, purchasing had to buy more inventory than was needed for the specific sale. Purchasing was not alarmed by this since the sales department always made an effort to get rid of the inventory. But it took time. To improve the speed with which the sale could be made, the sales department frequently gave "extra dating"— that is to say it agreed with the customer that he could hold up on the payment of his order for a specified period of time, frequently ninety days. Even when the sales department was successful in selling the excess inventory, it did not necessarily receive cash for that sale for a considerable period of time. Now there were two questions to be asked.

f.1. Why did the sales department sell items not in inventory in the first place?

The answer turned out to be simply that no one had told it why it should not. It sold whatever the market wanted and paid little heed to what the factory had in stock. The action in this case was to show it the harm done by selling items that had to be specially manufactured rather than selling items already in stock. No sooner did the sales department appreciate the gravity of its actions than it made an enormous effort to sell only those items in stock. Generally, it was successful and half the problem was solved.

f.2. Why was extra dating necessary?

The answer was that competition typically gave extra dating. However, after a discussion between the president of the company and the sales manager, it was concluded that, instead, a cash discount could be given. This action was taken immediately and as a result there was an immediate reduction in the level of outstanding accounts receivable.

As a result of these two answers, the rate of increase of the company's profit from operations showed a slight slowdown as sales growth slowed. More than offsetting this, however, interest expense declined as the company's cash position improved dramatically. Most important, of course, was that the improved cash position allowed the company to stay in business.

2. The second step, once the problem has been thought through, is to make sure that all people involved understand it in the same way. If left to themselves, it is amazing how frequently different people will reach different understandings of the same problem. This especially is true where two different viewpoints exist, as, for example, those of the factory manager and the sales manager. As an illustration of how such different viewpoints can color understanding, let us look again, in tabular form, at one of the examples above. A possible thought sequence might look like this:

Sales Manager	**Factory Manager**
a. Slow deliveries.	**a.** Slow deliveries.
Why?	Why?
b. Shortage of inventory.	**b.** Long inventories but the forecasts are always wrong so we have the wrong inventory on hand.

Why?

c. The forecasting system is incorrect.

Why?

d. The historical data is wrong.

Why?

e. Because the historical data is based on the previous data, which was also wrong.

Solution:
Have sales and marketing do the forecasts, at least for a while.

Why?

c. Sales always sells the wrong merchandise.

Why?

d. Because of a fundamental lack of discipline in the sales department.

Why?

e. That's just the way sales people are. ("They need a new sales manager. I could show them a thing or two.")

Solution:
Fire the sales manager and have the factory manager control the sales department!

Obviously the problem has to be very carefully explained by the manager in charge or, if the problem is sufficiently widespread, by the president of the company. But whoever the responsible man is, after he has thought the problem through to its real heart, he must then explain to all the participants precisely what the problem is, how it is derived and what simple actions are needed to resolve it. *The second principle of action is to explain what is going on and why.*

3. The third step is the solution to the problem. Dozens of books talk about the solution to the problem as if it were the main activity of life and of business life in particular. But it is not. Indeed, the solution to a problem, as I hope I have indicated, is one of the simpler parts of the anatomy of action. *Thus, the third principle of action is that once the problem is clearly defined in terms of a simple action, its solution is usually simple to understand.* Only on rare occasions is it intellectually difficult to solve the problem once you have defined it completely and explained it clearly.

Theodore Levitt of the Harvard Business School emphasized that the question of "what our business should be" is a vitally important part of the solution to business problems. He believed, presumably, that this is a very difficult question to answer; I think not. Indeed, it seems to me that it is essentially an irrelevant question. "What should our company be?" may be answered many ways. One choice cannot be proven to be better than another. The railroads chose nothing—that was clearly wrong. They could have chosen transportation with emphasis on mass and gone into the air cargo business; or they could have emphasized transportation with the emphasis on the individual and started producing automobiles. It ends up being a choice of what the overachiever "believes in."

However, there are problems which, while they are easy to solve in theory, require a considerable measure of motivation or leadership to resolve. Thus, the techniques making up the anatomy of action include those techniques which are effective in motivating men in business situations.

4. Motivation is the fourth step. In one sense, it is the most important part of the anatomy of action, for the fourth principle of action states: *Nothing will happen if there isn't somebody who wants to make it happen.*

Elsewhere in this book I have charted the overall aspects of motivation and tried to define some of the differences which exist in this respect between the ordinary and the overachieving businessman. Here, therefore, I would like simply to summarize some of the specific leadership techniques which are worth applying in those instances where a problem is to be solved and action is to be achieved. There are four such techniques which seem to me to be more important than all the others. They are:

a. Understanding and "feedback." One of the most dramatic facts about human communication is that it is so frequently ambiguous and ineffective. Time without number, two people believe that they have accurately understood what each has said only to discover later that their misunderstanding was almost complete. Sometimes it is possible to write whole agreements with which both parties agree—even though a fundamental disagreement between the parties persists. I suspect that this was Henry Kissinger's technique when he was able to make an agreement in writing between North Vietnam and the United States to settle the Vietnam War. The agreement exists but it is obvious that neither party ever had any willingness or even ability to live according to the same terms. The Americans did what they wanted and withdrew their troops, understanding that thereby the war would end. The North Vietnamese did what they wanted and conquered the South. Yet apparently both sides acted according to their understanding of the agreement.

In the business world it is more usual for an agreement to be useful if it is adhered to than if it is ignored. To make sure that understanding is as complete as possible, especially if the agreement is a casual, everyday one, it is usually helpful to use the technique of "feedback." Let me give you an example.

Statement of sales manager to salesman: "I think it might be a good idea, Mr. Smith, if you tried to step up the number of calls per day you are making. At the moment you're making an average of ten calls per day. Would you be good enough to set your sights on an average of eleven calls per day."

Feedback A: "I certainly will consider that possibility, Mr. Jones, and I'll let you know what parts of my in-store activity I would have to give up in order to increase the number of calls."

Feedback B: "I have considered that. I believe it would be impossible."

Feedback C: "Yes, sir, I will call on eleven stores per day from now on."

Obviously three different feedbacks have been received as a result of three different understandings by the salesman. In the first case he thought he was being asked for an honest evaluation of whether an increase in calls was desirable. In the second instance he felt the questioner was asking his opinion, not issuing a directive. In the third case, the salesman evidently felt that he was the recipient of an order from his boss.

Generally speaking, such "feedback" is enormously helpful because the first communicator can find out immediately whether his communication has been read the way he meant it. In the above example, the sales manager could easily have told either of the first two respondents that they misunderstood and what he meant was that they should make eleven calls. Alternatively, had he not meant that, he could have said to the third respondent, "Wait a second; before you increase your number of calls, I would like to know what you have to give up in order to be able to do that."

b. The second basic technique of leadership for action is to make the job fun. I realize that such a statement sounds almost puerile. It is not the less true for that.

Overachievers are typically liked because it is fun to participate in action. Or, as Ogden Nash put it:

> *No, you never get any fun*
> *out of the things you haven't done.*

I suspect that many people rarely have any fun in this world. Indeed, the most notable thing about Robert Townsend's book, *Up the Organization,* is that it shows that its author obviously made Avis, of which he was president, a thoroughly entertaining place to work. While he was there, Avis benefited from some remarkable achievements.

Humans are easily bored but they find it an unpleasant sensation. Since most people cannot overcome boredom alone, they will follow far the leader who can do it for them. The achiever who can make the world stimulating and fun for his subordinates can turn himself rapidly into an overachiever.

c. The third of this simple list of the four motivation techniques which form part of the anatomy of action is honesty and fairness. It is the willingness and the courage to let people know where they stand. Courage is frequently an important aspect of it. One of the more difficult tasks for most executives is to tell an employee (perhaps an employee who has become a friend) that he is not performing up to the standard the job requires or worse, that he is performing so badly that he has to leave the company. That, for most of us, is a heart-wrencher. But it is, I believe, essential. Indeed, it seems to me that the most important practical reason for telling people honestly where they stand is that to do so is the only way through which a feeling of true job security becomes possible. Where a company habitually demotes or fires people without telling them well in advance where they stand and what must be their fate if they cannot improve, then those who remain can never be sure that they are safe. Unless he is an overachiever of great courage, a man will not dare to create action unless he can be certain that he will keep his job as long as he does it well, and unless he knows clearly from day to day where he stands. Few men are willing to stick their necks out and make things happen if they know or fear that the first time something goes wrong they will be out of work. They know that the risk of something going wrong is far higher where there is constant striving for action than where the *status quo* is acceptable. (Obviously I mean only the risk of something going *visibly* wrong; for in inaction there is almost a certainty that the basic path is wrong.)

d. The final ingredient in leadership for action is the "you can do it" approach or, as I designate it for myself, the "Bruce's Spider Syndrome." (Robert the Bruce, you may recall, gathered the courage to persevere yet one more time in his fight against the English by watching a spider fall repeatedly from the ceiling and then climb laboriously back up its thread. Eventually the spider made it. In the short run so did Bruce.)

5. Creativity is the fifth step. However, in order to understand the application of creativity to the business world it is necessary not only to consider the meaning of creativity itself, as we will do elsewhere in this book when we discuss the power of an idea, but even more importantly it is necessary to define the difference between innovation and invention. Where the effectiveness of institutions, particularly business institutions, can be evaluated by the amount of achievement (be the amount in dollars, brownie points, or whatever other goal is set), then a change in the method designed to improve the amount of the achievement is an innovation.

In concrete terms it was innovative when the personnel manager of Helena Rubinstein decided to do away with most of the private secretaries and have the work done in a central "work-processing center." He thereby succeeded in getting more typing done at less cost. Whether measured in terms of dollars or measured in terms of output—the only two criteria of measurement which could have applied—he provided a different and in this case a better "economic satisfaction," i.e., he innovated.

It is of course a moot point whether it would be fair to call a negative innovation—that is, one which reduces the amount of economic satisfaction—an innovation. Technically I suppose it would be, but the definition is hardly useful. I am tempted (as e.e. cummings might have done) to coin the word "unnovation."

Invention is something quite different. It is rarely useful as the solution to a problem for it represents not the realignment of the existing but rather the development of the new. As such it is much more likely to give rise to problems then to solutions. Leonardo da Vinci, and much later the Wright Brothers, did not invent the plane in order to solve a problem. They invented it merely to invent it. The problems that they caused range from the phenomenon of "jet lag" to the equally traumatic experience of losing one's baggage at Kennedy Airport during rush hour. One might define the difference between innovation and invention by explaining that innovation is needed in order to find one's baggage and keep it under some degree of control, while invention is needed in order to create a new type of flexible material strong enough to avoid its almost immediate destruction by the automatic baggage handlers. *The fifth principle of action is that finding a better way makes things happen.*

6. The sixth and final step is fostering the spirit of determination, the unwillingness to admit easily to impossibilities. We are all taught from the womb to recognize the stringent limitations of our difficult world. How can a baby, vainly struggling against its swaddling clothes, be other than frustrated and convinced of its mortality? How can that baby, after being symbiotic with its mother for months, suddenly be left screaming and alone for an interminable twenty minutes without being convinced of the impossibility of most things? How can a schoolboy, unable to understand calculus and facing the idiotic question "What don't you understand?" learn more thoroughly of his own limitations? And yet we ask the adult facing a new and unattempted task to be open-minded and to consider that its achievement is possible.

It is the ability to overcome or to ignore his inevitable perception of his own limitations which differentiates the overachiever more clearly from his fellow man than any other quality. *The final principle of action is that reluctance to accept the impossible is the strongest way to lead men to action.*

The Overachiever
as Catalyst

Intrinsically, ideas have little value. It is only when they are implemented by determined men that they become influential.

The overachiever is not necessarily the man who creates an idea; but he is the man fortunate and bright enough to recognize it. Louis Pasteur said that "fortune favors the prepared mind." The overachiever is prepared to expand an idea, nurture it, strengthen it, make it practical, implement it, and ultimately force it upon the awareness of the world. An idea thrown out to an unappreciative audience or written in a file memo has as little value as would the music issuing from an expensive radio on a deserted island.

John Maynard Keynes wrote in *The General Theory of Employment, Interest and Money:*

> *The ideas of economists and political philosophers, both when they are right and when they are wrong, are more powerful than is commonly understood. Indeed, the world is ruled by little else. Practical men, who believe themselves to be quite exempt from any intellectual influences, are usually the slaves of some de-*

*funct economist. Madmen in authority, who hear voices
in the air, are distilling their frenzy from some academic scribbler of a few years back.*

At first sight Keynes's view would seem to be entirely at odds
with my conviction that ideas alone are of little importance. Not
at all. For the implication of Keynes's words is that the ideas are
influential only when, finally, they are activated by some practical man or, yes, by some madman in authority, who pushes them
into the practical world where their influence can be felt and
where, depending on their merit—and indeed the merit of their
sponsor—they do good or harm. I have no doubt that Mr. Keynes
would have agreed that for every idea which has been pushed
into the world by some great achiever there must be a million
which have remained mere academic scribblings. The first push
that most ideas, even great or world-moving ideas, must enjoy
is the renown of being published. They must be published
before they may even exist. Only if they experience existence
can they move to the next and definitive step, which is implementation. Obviously, publication does not mean in printed
book or article, it means merely the establishment of the idea in
some formal way comprehensible to others. Writing, because it
is the most durable of the communication techniques, is the
usual conveyance for an idea, but the concept which is "renowned in song and fable" may be just as potent.

   We do not have a Polaroid camera because Edwin Land had
the "idea" that it would be nice to have a camera that developed
its own film. That was an idea that millions of people had every
time they sent their film away to be developed. We have the
camera not because of the idea, which in any case Dr. Land
ascribes to one of his children, but because he was the sort of
activist who would not settle for the mild complaint: "I wish I
didn't have to wait a week to get my film developed." Instead,
he immediately started on the creation of a camera that could
develop its own film. We have the Polaroid camera because
Land was successful, both technically and commercially, in in-
venting, manufacturing, and selling the Polaroid camera.

Surely, Hugh Hefner's "idea" that young and well-developed girls are sexy had occurred to other young men. The difference between all those and Mr. Hefner was that he took his idea and turned it into a magazine. He published pictures of the nubile creatures. He put into words the new thoughts about sexual freedom that were rushing through his contemporaries' heads and called them the *Playboy Philosophy*. He persuaded major marketing companies who had been unwilling to advertise their products in "girlie magazines" that *Playboy* was not one of these, and attracted vast quantities of advertising. He opened first one and then a whole string of Playboy clubs where men could gawk at the pretty girls but where touching (and therefore the sort of trouble at home that would have cut drastically Mr. Hefner's potential clientele) was not allowed. The difference between Mr. Hefner and the rest of the world was not in his idea. The difference was that he created an empire while the rest of us merely swiveled our eyeballs.

Sometimes clever business ideas or new product ideas, large or small, seem to scintillate and sparkle. Even these, however, are valueless in themselves. To have life they must be implemented.

Roy Anthony is President of Marketing Innovations Inc., a company specializing in the creation of new product ideas. In 1967 he approached Philip Morris to say that he and his organization were supremely talented in this field. The point he kept emphasizing was that his ideas were practical.

"You're quite right," he said, "anyone can develop interesting new product ideas if he is not constrained by the practicalities of implementing them. But my ideas work. Indeed, my greatest pleasure is to make ideas work in the face of apparently insuperable limitations."

"In der Beschrankung zeigt sich erst der Meister," said Goethe, meaning that the discipline of imposed limitation is needed to allow the real master to be recognized. The man talking to Anthony at Philip Morris decided to impose some limitations:

"I'll give you a problem to solve," he said. "But I don't think you can help." He was anxious to be rid of him, but since he was committed, he continued: "Lifesavers are known as the candy with the hole and we cannot make a piece of hard candy with a hole, even a triangular piece with a square hole, without facing a lawsuit. But to compete successfully against Lifesavers, we'll need a piece of candy that looks as large, but contains no more candy than they do —and without a hole."

The demand seemed definitively impossible. Only a piece of candy with a hole in it could possibly fulfill these geometric requirements. It seemed inevitable that Roy would retire in disarray.

Quite the contrary. It took him just ten seconds to arrive at a perfect solution: "Put two holes into it," he said. And then, for good measure, he added: "And call it Buttons."

It was a small but perfect idea and Roy was hired on the spot. During the time he worked for Philip Morris, Roy came up with several other ideas, some of which became reality and were widely marketed. But that first idea, for all its apparent brilliance, was a poor one: it simply would not work because, as was discovered, a piece of candy with two holes in it breaks in the manufacturing process. They never could make Buttons. Perhaps someday someone will overcome the manufacturing problems and knock Lifesavers off their pedestal. If so, it will be he who makes the fortune—and who richly deserves credit for the idea. He will have made it *work*.

Only ideas that are made to work are remembered, or are worth remembering. They are conceived in any field, from finance to advertising, from politics to new product development. They have no more life of their own than ideas that fail; but they are given life by someone and so live.

In late 1969, I wanted to buy the Mason, Au and Magenheimer candy company, makers of Mason Dots and Mason Mints among other products, from Sidney and Archie Mishkin who also owned the Bayuk Cigar Company. Sidney had acquired Mason some years earlier for Bayuk but had lost interest in the candy industry and wanted to sell it. Unfortunately, the company for whom I wanted to buy Mason did not have enough money to make the acquisition.

"We'll give you $1 million of the purchase price in nonvoting preferred stock of our company which you can convert into voting common stock whenever you want," I offered.

Sidney agreed to this convertible preferred deal. "But the conversion price must be realistic," he insisted. "When I decide to convert my preferred stock to common I want to get about as much common stock as I would get right now for a million bucks."

It was a perfectly reasonable request. Unfortunately, it was one I could not accept. My company's stock was selling at what appeared to be a depressed price. Thus, giving away $1 million worth of preferred stock which could be converted into our common stock at its then market price would have given the Mishkins more of our common stock than my Board of Directors was willing to allow. We had reached an impasse.

Suddenly, I saw a solution. "I will give you a preferred stock which is convertible into one million dollars' worth of common stock at market price *every day*," I said.

Sidney looked rather surprised and thought awhile. "But then there is never a day when it is worth my while to make the conversion," he said eventually. "After all, as long as I hold the preferred stock I get dividends which you will not be paying on the common. And if I can convert at market price every day, there can never be a day when the conversion price is better than the market. There can never be a day when I can realize an immediate profit."

"True," I replied. "But there is never a day when you could not, if you wanted, obtain stock of our company worth one million dollars on the open market. And for my part, I don't have to look forward to the likelihood of my stock being excessively diluted."

My idea had eliminated the impasse. The deal was made based on this simple but, as far as I know, novel form of handling preferred stock. *It was an idea of value because it worked.*

Mary Wells had just founded her new advertising agency, Wells Rich Greene. In fact it had opened its doors in a hotel suite only about a week earlier. But already Philip Morris had given Mary the trial account of a low-selling but high prestige cigarette brand, Benson and Hedges, which was about to be introduced in a 100 mm. length. Pall Mall was expanding with such a new length and Philip Morris felt that it, too, should explore this new market.

I was half a minute late for the inaugural luncheon feting Mary Wells's entry into the Philip Morris family, with the result that I found myself forced to sit in the "hot" seat. Joseph Cullman III, head of Philip Morris and the host of this luncheon, naturally sat at the head of the table; Mary, as the honored guest, sat on his right; and I, as the tardy one, got the only chair left, which was at Joe's left.

Joe Cullman knew just what he wanted for the Benson and Hedges' advertising. He came to Philip Morris when that company acquired the Benson and Hedges Company, of which he was then president, and he was inordinately proud of the Benson and Hedges' name.

"I'd like a tall, regal girl as our spokesman," he explained firmly to Mary. "And I want her to announce our pride in bringing out a new, longer cigarette under the old and renowned name of Benson and Hedges." As Mary winced, he added: "And since the new package will be all gold, I think the girl announcing it should be in a gold dress."

"Yes, I quite agree that we need something nifty, something that consumers can enjoy and respond to," Mary said. She was not agreeing that it should be any tall girl in a gold dress!

"Like an attractive girl in a gold dress," Joe repeated very firmly.

I tried to interject some appropriate small talk to forestall the argument that I was certain was about to erupt. I was unanimously ignored.

"Maybe we could make people smile and love our cigarette," Mary said.

"We should show how proud we are to have given them such a fine product," Joe contradicted.

I squirmed and promised myself I would never arrive late again.

Fortunately, Mary was magnificent. She gave not an inch, but neither did she seem to fight. The luncheon concluded in harmony. I sighed with relief and fled.

I did not realize how magnificent she had been, however, until I happened to meet Joe in the passageway later that afternoon.

"Peter," he called to me. And then, as I approached, he said in a puzzled but somewhat dangerous voice: "Tell me, was Mary Wells disagreeing with me?"

I don't remember what I said, but I certainly did not answer his question. If he didn't realize how fundamentally different Mary's view was from his, I certainly was not going to be the one to enlighten him.

A while later, Mary Wells's agency recommended the now-famous advertising campaign based on the idea, "Oh, the disadvantages of Benson & Hedges." It was with undiluted admiration that I heard that Mr. Cullman had accepted the campaign without reservation and without hesitation. It takes a leader of real insight to change his mind so completely.

The advertising was, of course, excellent and it became wonderfully successful. But it is not primarily the advertising idea that I admire; my real admiration is for the determination of Mary Wells, and for Joe Cullman's open mind. Together, they made the idea work.

But my favorite example of an idea that had impact because it was made to work does not deal with the business world at all. It deals with, of all things, a young monkey who was observed on the little island of Koshima during the now-famous studies of Japanese rhesus-like monkeys conducted by two Kyoto University scientists, Kunichiro Itani and Masao Kawai. They were conducting experiments to see whether they could induce a group of between seventy and eighty monkeys to eat sweet potatoes. The potatoes were dropped onto a sandy beach near a stream not far distant from where the monkeys lived, and it was not long before all the monkeys were eating them. One monkey, however, a young female of only about eighteen months, decided that the sand that stuck to the potatoes was a nuisance. It took her only a short time to invent the idea of taking her sweet potatoes to the nearby stream and washing off the sand before she ate. But the real achievement lies in the fact that she did it so ostentatiously that, before long, the entire colony had copied this incredible forward leap. What an achievement!

By this time a new observer, Syunzo Kawamura, had taken over and had started to introduce another food unknown to the monkeys, namely, wheat. Again, there was no difficulty in persuading the monkeys to eat this new food, which they picked painstakingly out of the sand. All, that is, except the same female who had implemented the technique of washing the sweet potatoes.

She simply scooped up the wheat and the sand in handfuls and, taking the mixture to the stream, "panned" the sand away between her fingers. Again, it was not long before the rest of the community noticed and followed suit.

Few men, even among those who have reached the highest peaks of achievement, can match the achievement of this monkey.

I repeat: ideas, even excellent ideas, standing alone are cheap. It is one of the most difficult concepts to accept since we have all been taught, from early childhood, about the power of an idea. It is of course true that a business idea, indeed an idea in any field can, once implemented, have enormous power, enormous influence. But I emphasize again that it is the implementation, the correct, effective implementation by an activist, a doer, an achiever, that makes the difference between an idea of little value and one that moves the minds of men.

One can argue that this view has to be modified with respect to ideas on abstract subjects: philosophy, mathematics, painting. The argument would be that, since abstractions are by definition unimplementable in concrete terms, ideas in the abstract field would presumably be similarly difficult to implement: either all abstract ideas would be valueless, which is clearly nonsense; or ideas could be valuable without being implemented. The argument, however, is specious. First of all, of course, it hardly applies to the business world where abstractions have little place. More important, it does not even hold up with respect to truly abstract ideas. As regards philosophy and mathematics, they are not truly abstract. Christianity and communism can hardly be said to be abstract philosophies that were not implemented. And $E=MC^2$, leading as it did to the atomic age, cannot be said to have influenced the world in merely abstract terms. Even as regards painting, a more truly abstract medium, the fact remains that the ideas are valuable only to the extent that they are implemented. As John Ruskin put it in his book, *Modern Painters:* "He is the greatest artist who has embodied in the sum of his works, the greatest number of the greatest ideas." Ruskin did not say that he was the greatest painter who *had* the greatest number of ideas; rather that he was the greatest painter who *executed* them. That's the key.

Every man in business has seen ideas fail to bear fruit, and has seen them occasionally squashed or so emasculated that they stopped being ideas at all long before they were implemented. More often, most businessmen have seen ideas that were simply left to lie, sometimes for months or years, until someone else realized their potential.

A few years ago a man wanted to be employed to develop new products. "I invented the first cake mix," he explained proudly.

"What happened to it?"

"Well, Pillsbury brought theirs onto the market before I had a chance to do anything with mine," he said. "I also invented the first dry dog hamburgers which did not need refrigeration," he added.

"And what happened to that?"

"General Foods beat me out on that one."

The interview ended quickly!

Some ideas seem to grow on their own without any sponsor. They seem to spring from nowhere into full bloom. Perhaps they are ideas so great that they are irresistible. But I do not believe so. I think rather that they are ideas whose time has come, so that they are simultaneously accepted by many people and almost automatically implemented. "One should not underestimate ripeness as a factor facilitating discoveries which, as the saying goes, are 'in the air'—meaning, that the various components which will go into the new synthesis are all lying around and only waiting for the trigger action of chance or the catalyzing action of an exceptional brain, to be assembled and welded together," writes Arthur Koestler. It is not, in other words, that these "ripe" ideas are especially potent or have a "life" or a value of their own; rather it is that, because they are as ready to bursting as a ripe plum is full of juice, they are accepted not just by one but by many "actionists" simultaneously. They are implemented concurrently by many people and, since implementation is all, they obviously gain tremendously in potency from such widespread support.

More usually, however, when an idea seems to have grown on its own, it is simply because its sponsor, its implementor, is hidden. Even though it is a well-known human foible for successful brain children to spawn adoptive parents, quite often, try as they may, these false parents have difficulty in proving paternity. The impression often is given then that the idea has "immaculately" arisen. But I doubt it; always, I believe, there is a parent.

It was not the Colgate–Palmolive Company which introduced Colgate Dental Cream throughout the world—including many places where to market a toothpaste seemed preposterous—and, in the process, created healthier teeth in millions of kids, from Colombia to India, from Thailand to Spain. Rather, it was a series of dedicated individuals who were able to put that product into each local market with varying degrees of success, not based on the quality of the idea, but based on the quality of their implementation.

Implementing ideas is often a difficult task, for they can be very fragile; the newer they are the more pronounced their fragility. Often, these new ideas are diaphanous and hard to see very clearly. Occasionally, they are half-hidden by other less relevant matters which must be excised before their beauty can even be recognized.

It is in the context of their fragility that the difficulty of implementing ideas must be considered. New ideas are threatening even to the most open-minded of men. The "N.I.H." ("Not Invented Here") factor has become a cliché for describing how difficult it is for almost everyone to accept, let alone embrace with the enthusiasm needed for successful implementation, an idea not generated by himself; and few people are capable of generating their own ideas.

But if individuals have difficulty generating ideas and accepting them, then clearly groups have far more difficulty—for to move a group requires the consensus of a large number of individuals.

Whitby School in Greenwich was the first of the new wave of Montessori schools in America. It was founded some fifteen years ago by a group of highly innovative, creative parents. Today, it still attracts parents whose pride it is to be modern and highly receptive to new approaches. If any community can ever have an easy time accepting innovation, it should be the parent body of Whitby School.

At the start of each new academic year at Whitby there is a parent-teacher party. An excellent buffet and a generous bar is supplied by the parents; and the atmosphere is that of an informal cocktail gathering of sophisticated friends. At the end of supper the headmaster gives a talk. Jack Blessington, who was headmaster when my children attended Whitby, is one of the most astute educators and brilliant men I know. He is witty and forthright, innovative but sensible, experimental but careful.

In 1970, however, Jack was facing some unrest in the parent body, especially among the newer parents who were again worrying about two things: would Johnny learn how to read if he was allowed to walk around the classroom (as was standard at Whitby) rather than sit in tight rows and pretend to listen to teacher? And was it reasonable for boys and adult males to have long hair? These parental concerns were a constant undercurrent which flared up anew every few months. They were the symptoms of the adults' difficulty in accepting any educational style different from the one under which they had grown up. But on this occasion, the worst fears of the questioners were enormously magnified the moment they saw their headmaster. For, during the summer vacation, Jack Blessington had grown a luxurious beard!

It was still two or three years before beards stopped being unusual, and the conversation buzzed.

"*I* don't *mind*, of course, but really, a beard! For a headmaster!" The murmuring continued all through cocktails.

Finally, it was time for Jack to talk.

"I'm delighted to see you all again," Jack started. "It has been a difficult summer for me because I have been working in public education where any new idea is anathema. It is such a relief to return to you who are individually and collectively so bright and so open to innovation." He paused. Then, with a tiny twinkle, he continued. "Why, I had to grow this beard during the summer just to get the people I was working with used to any sort of change at all. Would you believe it, they were truly shocked by even the tiny idea that a headmaster can wear a beard!"

I do believe that the entire audience blushed!

If such a group of liberated parents have difficulty in accepting even such a small innovation as a beard, it is obvious that a large, relatively conservative business organization will have difficulty in acclimating itself to new ideas. Major corporations, particularly those who are not especially geared to the value of innovation, can be stifling. That any idea grows within some of them is a miracle against which the feat of the phoenix rising from the ashes pales in comparison. The decision-making process, the process by which ideas are implemented in certain large companies, is totally incredible. For example, Allen F. Demaree, writing in *Fortune* magazine of May 1970 about the AT&T Company, says, "Bell is a strange, perhaps unique, blend of independence and conformity . . . if you figure out a better way of doing something, forget it—they'd have to change the manuals." He is presumably right about Bell, but even though Bell may be an extreme case, I do not believe it is unique. Many other companies suffer from the problem of not having learned to accept innovation or improvement gracefully. Indeed, it is hard to believe how difficult it is, in certain extreme cases, to push through a new idea in some large corporations. Nevertheless, and at the risk of hopelessly violating John Gay's maxim, "lest men suspect your tale untrue, keep probability in view," I shall tell you the unvarnished truth of what actually happened to a young man some six years ago in one such company on a specific project.

At the time, he was a staff assistant, the lowest position on the management ladder. He had a very simple idea—one that was hardly worthy of the name. All he wanted to do was to change the usage instructions on the side panel of a box of one of the company's major brands.

"They're too complicated and dull; I could do far better," he declared.

So the young man talked to his boss, the assistant product manager, about this new project. The assistant product manager is second in command of the brand and works for the product manager. Together they are said to be the men who have charge of building the brand's sales and profits. (They do not, in fact, have any profit responsibility, as I shall discuss later, but they do have the *illusion* of having it.) Because this particular staff assistant was a persuasive fellow, he was able, more or less, to convince the assistant product manager that his idea was good.

"Put it into a document," he was told.

As soon as the document was completed, he presented it to the assistant product manager . . . who, skilled with red pencil, utterly annihilated the document in less than an hour.

The second writing took a week, and so did the third. However, after several further such bloody red-pencil baths, the document was finally ready (complete with artwork layouts, reasons, costs, proposed market research and half a dozen technical exhibits) to be handed to that august twenty-seven-year-old, the product manager. He, designated by the corporation's management as the executive responsible for the success or failure of the brand in question, spent an hour with an even sharper red pencil, destroying the document. It was rewritten several more times and a month later it was finally ready to be sent to the market research department for approval. The nominal job of the market research department is to determine what consumers think of products and their packaging and advertising. However, a not unusual function of the market research department in this large company seemed to be to delay decisions. Indeed, in this respect, the company, while perhaps extreme, was not unique. An alumnus of another great consumer-goods corporation, the Procter and Gamble Company, once said that in the entire eight years that he had worked there, he could not remember any service department ever approving anything without an argument the first time it was presented to them. As Archie once said to Mehitabel—and he could easily have been talking about several companies' market research departments—"procrastination is the art of keeping up with yesterday." In this particular instance, market research disapproved initially, but was eventually persuaded that, if certain changes were made, it would be willing to place its imprimatur on the plan for conducting market research on the new packaging instructions. And so the proposal went on to the art department which, as you will have guessed, disapproved.

Surprisingly, the young staff assistant still had some spark and energy left. Thus it was that this document—ten pages long, including details on the type of market research to be done, rough art, legal clearance, endorsement from the research and development department (which had to approve the new instructions), advertising agency concurrence, financial implications—was submitted to the general products manager for whom the brand manager worked.

This man, whose title may be different in various companies, simply has the function of coordinating the efforts of several product managers. In this case, he took a little longer to read the document and he made slightly fewer red-pencil marks. But once again, the document landed back on the staff assistant's desk for rewriting. Ultimately, it proceeded "up the ladder" yet again until, finally, it had the approval of the general products manager. He sent it with his covering note to the director of marketing of the division.

The director of marketing in this particular company sometimes made further corrections, sometimes he did not. His seemed to be the first level of command which, according to the rules of the game, did not *have* to make corrections. In this particular instance, the director of marketing was in agreement with the proposal and the document was sent forward to the general manager of the division. This is the man whose job it is to plan and coordinate the business path for a group of products. His is the first executive level with responsibilities that encompass manufacturing as well as marketing; he also usually sits in a quiet office. (The offices of all the other people we have met so far on this mammoth project have been vibrant with noisy visitors and frantic typists.)

The general manager conferred on the important subject of this packaging change with a number of other heads of department. For example, he discussed the matter with the head of market research and the head of the legal department. He also met the head of the art department at lunch and mentioned it to him. You may note a certain similarity between this description of the general manager's task and the task which the staff assistant had already performed. You are correct in so noting, for the tasks are essentially identical, although carried out at different levels.

We are now very close to the decision point. Finally, the document, complete with samples of finished art, and boasting a separate cover document from the occupant of each ladder rung, was ready to be presented to the vice president. The vice president is, of course, a senior executive who, in most companies, has the ultimate decision-making authority on all but the most important decisions. He may well be looked upon with some degree of awe by a young staff assistant.

Naturally, the vice president was a very busy fellow and didn't have time to go into all this nonsense about the packaging change. All he knew was that the brand was selling very nicely and that it hardly seemed worthwhile to take any risks by making some minor changes thought up by some obviously wet-behind-the-ears staff assistant. So he simply wrote "No" in large letters on the outer document—and that seemed to be the end of that!

"First, I nearly shot myself," the young man recalls. "Then I nearly shot him!"

Instead, he summoned up his determination for one final effort and resubmitted the entire wad of documents with a rather passionate covering memorandum. The vice president, probably fed up with hearing about the subject, changed his mind and wrote "OK, Good," across the top of it. Some months later, the product had new and undoubtedly improved usage instructions.

If my description of what it took to get new usage instructions approved at this particular company is even half-right—and I again assure you that I am not exaggerating—it is hard to imagine how difficult would be the task of obtaining approval for a *real* idea. Can you imagine what an ugly stump of the original brilliant thought would be likely to remain after all those management layers had wrought their "improvements"; and all those rewrites had mutilated the idea; and all that glue of boredom had overwhelmed its gossamer beauty? And yet, the company is not badly run; often excellent new ideas, neither stunted nor deformed, emerge from it.

Someone once said that a camel is really an airplane designed by a committee. I can only add that, considering the way that some committees or corporate organizations attack and destroy new thought, it is amazing that anything half as good as a camel could possibly emerge. It seems to me that genuine ideas containing an element of novelty and invention should have about as much chance of survival in many massive business organizations as do snowflakes in August. And yet, survive they do.

Admittedly, some of the "ideas" which survive in today's big organizations are not ideas at all: they are mere truisms with neither flare, invention, nor guts. At their worst, they grow, like cuckoos, by throwing out the real ideas and gobbling up their nourishment. They are the blunt and obvious thoughts which no amount of kneading and squeezing can destroy. They are the "ideas" of copying today what your competitor did yesterday; or of bringing out a giant, economy version of the package you already have; or of cutting your price in order to sell more. They are occasionally good business moves, but they are hardly ideas. They are the new product ideas that consist of no more than the assembly of the same old ingredients in yet another version of the same old way. The reason that *it is almost traditional in the marketing field to expect only one new product in five to succeed,* is that at least three of these "new" products are not really new at all, but merely warmed-over versions of old ones.

Yet, I repeat, many genuine ideas, often brilliant ones, which move the minds or change the lives of men, do emerge. They do so, I believe, because they are sponsored by some determined man who made up his mind to protect and push through an idea —no matter its quality. Supported by a good man, a mediocre idea will have more success than will a brilliant idea that is unsupported.

I am not trying to say that all ideas are of equal value. Some are adequately implemented, but simply do not work: if they are new products, people don't want them; if they are new plays, people don't attend them—even though Clive Barnes thinks they should; if they are new magazines, like Hugh Hefner's or Huntington Hartford's on show business, people don't read them; and if they are new politicians, people don't believe them. After all, Columbus might have implemented his idea perfectly and sailed westward—only to fall off the edge of the world!

The "great" idea is indeed rare. Not many men can generate an idea such as mass production, as did Henry Ford. He had a genius so great that it almost seems like blindness. Marshall McLuhan puts it:

> Henry Ford turned to making history by scrapping the agrarian world around him. He was one of the greatest creators of new social clothing and service environments. While ordering every pattern of the contemporary world and of history, he resolutely averted his gaze from the past and present alike . . . he was ahead of his time. He could afford to junk history, since he was history.

Nor could many men develop the complicated business idea of the computer as an industrial tool as did Watson of IBM.

The ideas of men like Ford and Watson are ideas of brilliance; their implementation is genius. I am convinced that it is only the man who can both generate a good idea and implement it who can be called a genius. Indeed, I have a sneaking suspicion that many of the "best" ideas never see the light of day. Lots of poor or at least limited ideas have made it, simply because they were picked up by some snarly overachiever who simply would not quit. But just imagine if that same man had chanced upon a really *good* idea; imagine what sort of success William Wrigley might have had if his idea of chewing gum had not been innately disgusting!

When I think of all the ideas which never found a sponsor, I am irresistibly reminded of part of Aldous Huxley's "The Fifth Philosopher's Song":

> *A million, million spermatozoa,*
> *All of them alive:*
> *Out of their cataclysm but one poor Noah*
> *Dare hope to survive.*
> *And among that billion minus one*
> *Might have chanced to be*
> *Shakespeare, another Newton, a new Donne—*
> *But the One was Me.*

If one man creates the idea, and another implements it, I suggest that it is the implementor who is the greater achiever. Certainly, he is the more rewarded.

A small company called Porosan has, since 1935, invented: the first porous oil-containing ball bearings; the first self-sterilizing paint; the only analgesic bandage; the first plastic wood; the first dried potatoes; the first in-home fruit-preserving technique; the first method of perfuming plastics; the first dry room-deodorizer; the first self-expanding curtain rods; the first way of insulating and rust-protecting factory and home pipes with a simple self-hardening plastic; the first . . . the list is almost endless and flabbergasting.

Moreover, these were new and brilliant ideas. They were not simply remakes of old thoughts or variations upon old themes. The company developed dozens of patents in at least ten different fields. It owns at least a half-dozen unexploited patents, and many more that are pending, that at this very moment have been neither implemented by Porosan nor sold to anyone else.

Yet few of these ideas, old or new, have been pushed through to completion by the Porosan company. Instead, Porosan typically chose to sell each of them

in its early stages to some major company, where the ideas either fell dead—
or fell into the hands of some corporate overachiever and prospered mag-
nificently. Indeed, some of the Porosan ideas have had a major world-wide
influence. One of them, a technique for reducing the flammability of wooden
airplanes, helped England withstand the early days of the German air onslaught
in World War II. Another, the in-home fruit-preserving technique, helped England to live healthily through food shortage and rationing. Yet another, "peat
pots," a technique for making flowerpots which, when planted outside, slowly
disintegrate to fertilize the plant, made a major change in the horticulture and
truck-farming industries of the world.

The founding genius of Porosan has never been widely acclaimed. He has
lived well and marvelously happily all of his life and that, of course, is an
achievement in itself. But because his ideas have been implemented by others
and not by him, others have reaped the main rewards. That, I believe, is as it
should be.

The managements of most large corporations do, of course,
recognize the essential importance of ideas, of new approaches,
of improvement. But they face the same problems in having
innovation accepted as do their most conservative of employees
—at least in kind if not in degree. For any human organization,
however open-minded to innovation and invention its leaders
may be, will suffer from the same problem: change is uncomfortable. It is, I think, innate in our psychological make-up that
change is repugnant. Even if it is made as palatable as possible,
it remains difficult. Anyone who has seen a child worry about
going to school in a shirt that looks different from his usual one,
or has seen a young wife worry herself to a frazzle at the thought
of moving, or has seen the agony of a young executive trying to
decide whether to accept a new, apparently better job, even
within his own company, will have an understanding of the
difficulty of change.

So we face a very fundamental question: how is it possible that
great corporations do, in spite of the human tendency to resist
new ideas, still develop so many good ones? How is it that, in
spite of all the difficulties, quite frequently a new idea emerges
somewhere in a giant company, stretches its beautiful and evi-

dently not so fragile wings and slowly, falteringly, but successfully grows in size, strength, and definition until it turns into a genuinely new product and then into a profit center and occasionally even into a whole new and profitable division?

On a very limited front, why is it that Virginia Slims, the first thin cigarette made especially for women, rapidly became a commercial success whereas any number of other brands experimented with by Philip Morris never saw the light of day? Why is it that Erin Gems, the marvelous new candy product created by the Ireland–America Candy Company, started off gloriously and then suddenly shriveled and died right in the middle of its early marketing success? Why has Airwick successfully introduced a dry room-air-freshener with great commercial success while no one has introduced a dry room-vaporizer even though there is an excellent one being offered by its inventor at this very moment?

The answer in these instances—and in virtually every similar case—lies with the people involved. Obviously, you cannot call Virginia Slims a great idea; and yet it is a commercially successful one. The reason is that one overachiever, Jack Landry of Philip Morris, decided that this was an idea he would nurture. He was less interested in other new Philip Morris brands—and, as a result, they didn't make it. Erin Gems got off the ground because Sidney Feltenstein, who was then director of marketing for the firm selling this brand, loved it. When he left to run the biggest division of Dunk 'n' Donuts, Erin Gems seemed to lose their sparkle. Today, as far as I know, they are no longer available on the market. They were an excellent product, excellently packaged, and excellently advertised—but they ceased to exist. They lost their sponsor and that, I believe, is the only possible explanation for how, in that case, defeat was snatched from the jaws of victory. Let us hope that the Airwick story does not end in the same way. The company is still small, but has just been acquired by a giant company which declares it is determined to make it grow. The question is: will the Airwick executives continue to have that drive to achievement now that they have sold the company? Or will they slow down, cash in their stock options, take it easy and create a new products department instead of new products?

The tenacity and tact needed by the man who has decided to push an idea through the slough of human resistance to eventual fruition must be great indeed. The overachiever's difficulties, while they may be eased by the support of a great organization dedicated to the successful introduction of new ideas and new products, nevertheless may make the Progress of Pilgrim seem almost unchallenging. Above all, it is in those frequent cases where there is a constant wearing down of his determination that even the stubbornest corporate businessmen may be defeated. Stephen Spender wrote a poem called "What I expected, was" which, in four of its lines, summarizes the problem:

> *What I had not foreseen*
> *Was the gradual day*
> *Weakening the will*
> *Leaking the brightness away.*

It takes a great deal of resiliency to continue to push an idea with enthusiasm in the face of constant, gentle negativism and to avoid such "brightness leaks." In a sense, even violent opposition is better than slow, molasses-like resistance, because strong opposition can be grappled with and perhaps overcome, while reluctant, procrastinatory agreement is enervating in the extreme. To continue to push under these circumstances takes, I suggest, a corporate "bull," a stubborn, vigorous animal with its neck far out; a man with a dream; an overachiever. These are the men who push forward business organizations large and small. These are the men who are in demand. These are the men who succeed.

Procrastinations: The Bane of the Overachiever

"Defer no time, delays have dangerous ends," thunders Shakespeare and, "Never put off until tomorrow what you can do today," carps an unending series of schoolteachers. But organizations of people have a tendency to procrastinate. Certainly big business is no exception to this tendency. The overachiever in many corporations is beset by a vast variety of techniques of potential procrastination which he must learn to recognize and overcome in order to move forward effectively. Indeed, the ability of a man to overcome procrastinations may well be the measure of his ability to achieve. To recognize these delays and merely complain of them might be legitimate in a social critic but would be both useless and unacceptable in a businessman.

One of the most useful of the techniques of marketing, but also one which can lead to procrastination, is market research. It is difficult to overstate the importance and usefulness of good market research. It is impossible to make a decision about what two hundred million Americans or a hundred million Brazilians want, purely on personal judgment. Obviously, in order to get some understanding of the desires of any vast population, it is essential to choose a statistically valid sample of the population

—and then find out from them what they really want, not what you guess they want. I have no argument with market research per se. On the contrary, I am convinced that, without accurate market research, the manufacture and marketing of consumer goods would be very much less efficient than it is. On the other hand, I also know just how insidious a market research department can be in helping marketing functionaries do nothing; and even dynamic corporate organizations typically hide amid the branches of their organization charts a number of such sluggish people. *Market research is essential, yes; but where it is misused it can be one of the more debilitating forces in big business today.* Yet, it is such a logical necessity that even if it is conducted badly or slowly or employed to obtain irrelevant information, it is enormously difficult to object to. Who can argue with the need to ask women their opinion as to which of two packages they prefer? Who can gainsay the man who demands to have a statistically representative sample of housewives questioned as to their intent to purchase a new product? Who has the temerity to stand up and maintain that he is able to forecast accurately the opinions of consumers, in their millions, without the help of the market research department?

Many sorts of market research help the marketing man make the right decisions; others unfortunately tend merely to delay him. While I do not intend to describe and compare them all, a few examples should be useful.

One of the most popular and widely used techniques in market research is the "concept test." It takes many forms but in essence it always consists of describing the "concept" or idea of a new product and then asking a number of potential purchasers why they like or dislike it, as described, and whether or not they would buy it.

The first piece of concept research that I ever heard about was conducted by the young General Electric Company at a time when the electric refrigerator had yet to be introduced and the iceman still came regularly. G.E. asked women whether they would be interested in an electric icebox that kept cold all the time—without having to be fed ice every day, without drips, and without fuss. The answer was an overwhelming "No." Why, women wondered, would they have any use for such a newfangled gadget? It would be dangerous and expensive and noisy and ugly—and anyway, what would the poor iceman do if he had nowhere to take his ice? The research did not stop the introduction of the refrigerator, but it certainly caused delays.

That may have been the earliest concept research study. But I am reasonably convinced that few studies conducted later were any more accurate. People simply cannot *imagine* what they would buy; that is a theoretical question. It all depends, doesn't it? When the question is asked, probably by some earnest young man, they simply don't know.

First they try to be honest. "Well, I'm not really sure . . ."

"Yes, but what do you *think?*" the interviewer interrupts.

"Well, it depends on . . ."

"Of course, but if you had to make the decision right now?"

"My husband . . ."

"Yes, madam, but we are interested in *your* opinion," the young man insists.

After a while, the housewife starts to be embarrassed by her apparent indecisiveness. So, since she really doesn't know what *she* would buy, she casts herself into the role of an expert on *all* women and tries to imagine what other people would do. Thus, while concept research is done so that the marketing man need not try to predict the preferences of millions of consumers, all that it normally achieves is the transfer of his responsibility to 350 totally unequipped housewives. Is it any wonder that four out of five new products introduced into the market place after the most careful concept testing fail? Personally, as I have said before, I can barely conceal my amazement that one out of the five succeeds.

And is it any wonder that the introduction of a new product, at least in many companies, is a gigantic task which can take years to complete? To me it is a great compliment to the marketing process generally and to the overachievers in it in particular that our economy is fired and our population made happier and healthier by such a constant abundance of fine new products.

The concept test is not, of course, the only piece of research which may cause delay if not carefully watched. Another very widespread one is the use of advertising recall research to measure the selling effectiveness of a television commercial. In essence, every one of the many types of recall research conducted is similar: the commercial to be tested is shown to a limited television audience and then, some time later, members of that audience are interviewed to determine whether they remember the commercial and its main selling message or not.

As a way of memory- or comprehension-testing, the method is useful; and it may also be useful as a way of comparing two essentially similar commercials. But as a method of determining the over-all selling effectiveness of an advertising campaign it has little validity. Just consider: do you remember where you first learned the nursery rhyme "Jack and Jill went up the hill"? In all likelihood you do not; and yet you know the rhyme. Which merely proves the obvious, namely, that it is quite unnecessary to remember the source of information in order to assimilate that information. Let us assume that you believe General Motors cars rattle less than Fords. Certainly the belief is not based upon fact. First of all, you are probably not an engineer; second, you have not tried a representative sample of both makers' cars; and third, it is probably not true. It is just something you "know," something of which you are convinced. Most likely, it is something that you "heard." But whether you were told and have the information second- or third-hand, or whether you yourself saw an advertisement or television commercial which convinced you, this type of information is likely to have come originally from some form of advertising. The advertising has, of course, long since been forgotten; but the conviction remains and guides you in your choice of cars. Indeed, it could be argued that, if you recalled that it was a commercial from which your conviction stemmed, you might be less convinced. Obviously, I would not go so far as to say that an advertisement which you remember is always worse than one which you do not. I merely suggest that there is not necessarily a positive correlation between recall and sales effectiveness. And I suggest that here we have another example of how market research used incorrectly may cause delay by seeking to determine something that is not really worth knowing.

The really surprising thing about my statement that recall research often provides little meaningful information is that there is widespread agreement with me, especially among action-oriented marketing people. Yet such recall research continues to be conducted by many major companies as a "safety valve." As such, I suggest, it is more a procrastination, or a way to avoid a heart-wrenching decision, than it is a useful device. There are, of course, good ways to research the comparative effectiveness of commercials, as I shall mention later. But sometimes it is even better to put your judgment on the line and say "I know the commercial will sell goods. Let's go." That is often how the best of advertising campaigns, supported by the best of men, are launched. That, indeed, is a frequent approach of the overachiever.

Market research is used by every big corporation, sometimes on a huge scale. There are new, more sophisticated, and better ways of conducting it developed every day. But too much of it becomes a delaying technique and even, at its extreme, a shield for weak men to hide behind; then it is a barrier to those overachievers who have the courage and the need to get something done and who are willing to take the risks of being wrong.

The type of market research that can be the most helpful is always, in essence, the same. Instead of asking women: "What would you do if . . . ," you place them in the position of actually *doing* it, and then observe the results. For example, if you want to measure the selling effectiveness of an advertising campaign, you show a representative sample of consumers the campaign ads or commercials and then see whether they buy or not. It is the simplest of all rules to understand, and it is followed rigorously by several of the best and most dynamically led consumer-goods companies. For example, some companies conduct market research on advertising by parking a trailer in front of a shopping center and inviting women who are about to go shopping into the trailer to view a reel of TV commercials. Some of the women see several commercials, including the one to be tested; others see the same commercials, but without the one to be tested. All the women then proceed with their shopping. However, unknown to them, they are watched and their actual purchases monitored. The difference in purchase level between the women who saw the test commercial and those who did not is the measure of the effectiveness of the commercial. By comparing the test commercial's selling effectiveness under these circumstances with the results from many other commercials tested in the same way, a pretty good idea of its real selling effectiveness in the market place can be gained. Obviously, the techniques for selecting the respondents and for observing them are more sophisticated than I indicate here. Handling these details in the correct way makes all the difference. But the essence of the technique is as I have described it, and it is sound because it measures actual behavior in the real world.

Concept testing, if it is done right, works the same way. You do not ask women what they think. You place them in a position of *having to choose* which of several products to purchase—or of having to choose whether to buy or not—and then you observe what actually happens.

To summarize, the general rule is that good market research must observe *what* people do, not what they judge that others, or even they themselves, *would* do under theoretical circumstances. The problem is that it is sometimes very difficult to avoid placing consumers in such a theoretical position. For example, if you want to test the quality of a new product which is not yet on the market, you obviously cannot observe consumers purchasing it. Instead, you may have to give it to them to try on a test basis and then ask them what they think of it. Fortunately, in this case, you are asking the person to be an expert on something he really is expert about—himself. You are asking, "Do *you* like this product which I gave you to use, or not?" and the respondent knows the answer to that. He knows what he likes or dislikes, and he is therefore able and usually willing to tell you. Product tests of this sort are often useful pieces of research but, even so, one has to be careful since they too can be very misleading.

Some years ago a minor chewing gum brand had succeeded in attracting consumer attention as a result of some brilliant advertising, and it was starting to sell. However, it existed in only three flavors and they were so-called specialty flavors, that is, ones which only a minority of people really like. Most people who chew gum prefer one of the minty flavors, especially Wrigley's Doublemint. The company's management decided, therefore, that to be able to cut into Wrigley's market they would simply have to introduce a peppermint chewing gum.

"What we need is a better peppermint flavor than Doublemint in order to be successful," the marketing director announced to his research and development experts. "We know it's going to be tough, but we're assigning top priority to the project so that we can introduce our new gum before Christmas. We'll give it the code name of Triplemint." (As it turned out, Wrigley had registered that name decades before, brilliantly anticipating the inevitable!)

The R and D people did a superb job and investigated every sort of variation on peppermint. And each time they developed what they thought might be an improvement, they went to the market research people with it and asked them to find out what consumers thought.

"We are developing a new sort of peppermint flavor," market research explained to gum chewers across the United States. "What do you think of this one?" They then gave the respondent either a stick of Wrigley's wrapped in white paper or a similarly wrapped stick of the newly developed product.

Again and again the consumers preferred Wrigley's.

Finally, against the odds, research and development managed to find the better peppermint the management wanted. When the research results came in, even the secretaries were ecstatic. At last they had found it! Old Archimedes in his bathtub could not have been happier. A better peppermint flavor than Wrigley's! Individually, some of the employees were not all that impressed with the new flavor; to them, it tasted rather sharp. But the market research results seemed quite incontrovertible: they had a clear-cut win over Wrigley.

The company had been ready for months. All the marketing plans were waiting, the television commercials shot, the sales brochures printed. All the packing material had been designed and ordered. It took only a few weeks to open the test market. They chose Seattle as the test area.

Practically every executive in the organization visited the test market at least once in its brief life. Certainly no test has ever had more management attention. A better gum than Wrigley's! Inevitably, the result was that it did extremely well. Massive sales effort of this type always results in extra sales. After all, the local salesmen, with the eyes and the ears of the world upon them, were going to make extraordinary efforts. I'm sure that the sales people in that particular territory cashed in every favor they had collected over the years to get the sort of featuring and display they obtained. The gum was practically given away to consumers, so helpful and friendly was the retail trade.

One overachieving young salesman who had been with the company for only a few days when the test started decided that here was an opportunity to make an instant name for himself. His biggest account was a small drugstore. By dint of hard selling, he managed to persuade them to take ten boxes—that is, two hundred packs—of the new gum. Since the store probably had no more than two hundred customers a week, this was a large amount. Unfortunately, the young salesman did not quite understand the order form—and a week later the store owner was surprised to see ten *cases* of the new peppermint gum, each case containing twenty boxes, turn up at his delivery entrance. That was four thousand packs. How the salesman succeeded in persuading the storekeeper not to send the gum back I do not know. All I know is that in that store there was gum in the rafters! You have never seen so much gum. To go with the gum there were posters and display material, an enormous price cut on the gum and, for good measure, price features on all the other candy in the store. The kids were knee deep. The drugstore owner wasn't sure whether he was working on his first million dollars or going broke.

All in all, the test market of the new peppermint gum was a roaring success and "national expansion" took place in record time.

Nationally, the brand was a resounding failure. It was not quite so bad that it had to withdraw entirely from the market place, but it was almost that bad. The gum simply refused to sell. Moreover, as soon as the excessive sales effort in the test market stopped, so did the sales there. It was obvious that consumers simply didn't like the new peppermint gum very much.

Management searched a hundred different paths to try to find the answer until finally, almost in desperation, it decided to look at the market research results again: they were quite clear. Consumers preferred the new gum to Wrigley's when they were asked which of the two was the better peppermint gum. Suddenly the director of market research had a blinding flash of intuition. As fast as he could he mounted a new piece of research. "What flavor does Wrigley's Doublemint have?" he asked consumers.

"Oh, sort of buttery." "Spearmint!" "Peppermint with another sort of nutty taste mixed in." "I don't know, it's not like any other flavor that I know." "Well, they call it mint, but it's not like ordinary peppermint. It really isn't peppermint at all. I don't much like peppermint, but I love Wrigley's Doublemint."

And there they had it. They had produced a better peppermint than Wrigley —and everyone preferred Wrigley because it *wasn't* peppermint. Even the most carefully laid schemes of market research, like those of mice and men, "gang aft a-gley"!

Nothing I have said should be construed to suggest that I am not strongly in favor of conducting market research. I am. I believe in it. I am convinced that, correctly conducted, market research can greatly speed up the introduction of new products and can greatly reduce their failure rate. As Peter Drucker writes on the first page of his "how to" book, *The Effective Executive,* "the executive is, first of all, expected *to get the right things* done." I am sure that market research, conducted with discipline, can help him considerably to know what the right things are. It cannot, however, get them done for him.

There are many decisions which are quite obvious, and many others which, while not obvious, are obviously not important. To do market research on any such decisions is ridiculous.

The overachiever, anxious to get things moving forward, will be able to say "yes" and "no" to many of the decisions which come before him without resorting to market research.

"Should we conduct a piece of research on changing the package line for our chocolates?" the product manager wanted to know.

"Why are we changing?"

"Because Sears, which is our only large customer on this item, will not buy unless we make the change."

Market research was not, it seemed, absolutely essential in order to decide to make the change!

Moreover, the overachiever will be quite justified on many occasions in saying: "I don't know, but the change is so small or the alternatives are so similar that it really is not important. Let's decide either to do it or not and then go about our business without wasting further time." Yet, surprisingly, even apparently successful men in many different walks of life, including the business world, sometimes stand between similar alternatives agonizing and market-researching them into the ground.

The overachieving marketing man is the sort who seeks to limit his mistakes by research but who never seeks to substitute research for action. For him it is almost easier to say, "Let's do it," than to say, "Let's research it." And yet there are many occasions—the more, the more innovative and energetic the marketing leader is—where the answer to the question "Will this sell?" or "Is this an improvement?" must be: "I think so, but I don't know for sure. Let's market research it to find out."

In summary, then, the fundamental problem to be solved in order to make market research productive is to establish a simple way of making sure whether it is really needed or not. To do so, I suggest one simple rule: whenever any piece of research is recommended, insist that it be accompanied by a clear statement describing the action to be taken as a result of the research. It is surprising how often the "action" to be taken is something such as: "If the results show that the product to be tested is preferred, we shall consider . . ." For such request I suggest the rebuttal: "Consider now. *Then* do the research!"

Another dangerous technique of procrastination found frequently in the business world may be termed the "memo" or the "document."

A junior employee develops an idea and tells his boss about it. To describe it takes about ten minutes.

"Write it down in detail," the boss says. "Then I shall give it serious consideration."

Writing such an idea in detail involves gathering a bank of pertinent but not essential data. It involves several hours of mechanical writing or dictation, typing and retyping, formal clearance with other departments (who are admittedly in agreement with the general idea but who have to get into the details of the written document), and finally an hour or two of indexing, cross-referencing, and collating.

All of this is, of course, a very necessary effort as the first stage of the implementation of an idea in order to clarify its otherwise ill-defined facets. But it is generally quite unnecessary in order to understand the idea in principle.

When the document is completed, the young man takes it back to his boss who reads it carefully (which may take some time, particularly if he is inefficient) and then, without committing himself to anything, concludes that the memo could be even more clearly written. Obviously, this is the worst of circumstances, but it is not unrealistic.

One young woman, immediately upon leaving the university, joined a major marketing company and was assigned to work for a brilliant but inexperienced and rather Napoleonic boss. Her first written assignment was a note thanking the advertising agency for an interesting meeting and summarizing the major points that had been made during that meeting. Without exaggeration, she was forced to rewrite that letter seventeen times—she says she can still quote it today!

If the "memo" is an unfortunate technique of procrastination, let me assure you that, "Have you cleared this with Legal?" is a far more dangerous one. In modern American business legal departments have gathered enormous power, for laws are not only a means to enforce good conduct but are rapidly becoming a publicity platform for ambitious men. The standard thesis for the law used to be: *Salus populi suprema lex esto* (The safety of the people is the supreme law). But today, I believe, the law is too often used for the advantage of the politician or the consumerist (who may be the same person). It was not long ago that a politician, in order to make a name for himself, had to do little more than discover a communist. Today, fashions have changed. Now, in order to make a similar name, an unscrupulous politician can go far by finding a consumer product that he can claim to be dangerous, or an advertisement that he can claim to be untruthful.

Obviously, not all consumer advocates are mere publicity hounds; most are honest and helpful people. Nor does any man of integrity dispute the need for truth in advertising, not only in the United States where the law demands it, but in all those countries of the world where lies are legally permissible. The overachievers' view of advertising is, very simply, that lies are bad for business. More can be sold by making a good product and telling the truth about it than by trying to mislead consumers. Yet, as the result of the excesses of a few consumerists, it has become increasingly difficult in the United States to tell the truth in advertising. If you photograph whipped cream under the hot lights needed for filming, the whipped cream dries out very rapidly and doesn't look like whipped cream. The film that one would see on television, instead of showing a "truthful" picture of what whipped cream looks like, shows an "untruthful" picture. It used to be customary, therefore, to use mashed potatoes which, photographed under the same lights, happened to look exactly like real whipped cream. Thus, while the technique for recording the whipped cream on film was "untruthful," what actually appeared was a true rendition of what the product actually looked like. This was adjudged to be false advertising. On the other hand, before they were banned from television entirely, the cigarette companies were required not to use young actors in television commercials. Instead, some of them simply retained older actors who happened to photograph extremely young—and thus ran "truthful" advertising using thirty-five-year-old teen-agers!

The business problems that arise from this sort of governmental control need not be serious. They are merely annoying delays if the legal department is anxious for action. But if a legal department lacks its quota of overachievers, major corporate problems will probably result. Lawyers today have come to fill an "interpretation gap" that exists because government standards are severe but often not clearly defined. The widening of the gap requires experts who strive constantly to keep up to date on the current interpretation of government standards. These experts have come to be lawyers, who today are essential for deciding what is likely to be held truth and what falsehood in advertising.

Product safety is another area of enormous difficulty for the businessman under today's legal-political setup. Obviously, no man who is not truly sinful is likely to put a food product onto the market and feed it to his customers, his friends, and his children unless he is convinced that it is safe. On the other hand, there are some sinful men—and there are some benighted ones —who *would* put out products without due care and without due testing that might be truly dangerous. Moreover, without sufficient control, other things can go wrong. The thalidomide affair of some years ago, in which perfectly ethical companies marketed an anti-nausea drug for pregnant women which, as it turned out, deformed their unborn babies, is a case in point. There can be no doubt therefore that we require safety laws and controls.

But those laws can and in some recent instances appear to have become dramatically exaggerated. Were aspirin not yet marketed it might well fail to obtain a Food and Drug Administration clearance. After all, even though aspirin does an enormous amount of good for tens of millions of people, there is no doubt that to some, on some occasions, it does some harm.

In this area, as in truth in advertising, it is the lawyers who interpret the regulations, who become the "pre"-arbiters of safety and who help to determine what sort of testing needs to be done.

These are but two examples of the new involvement of lawyers in business, but they are involved in a hundred ways: acquisitions and restraint of trade, price fixing, union negotiations, fair and unfair employment practices, discrimination, women's rights, employment conditions, package instructions, ingredient copy on packages, product usage methods, tax matters (and more tax matters!), accounting principles, international financing, Security and Exchange Commission procedures, public reporting, public relations statements, annual reports and their content, employment contracts and the hiring and firing of key employees, secrecy agreements, industrial espionage, Washington contact, pollution, factory safety standards . . . the list is almost endless.

Charles Dickens wrote, in *Bleak House*, "The one great principle of the English law is, to make business for itself." The cynic might feel that in America today nothing is different in this respect. But whether or not business problems are lawyer-exacerbated (and I do not think that they are), the fact is that the modern businessman must place more and more reliance on his lawyers. In each of the cited areas, he must consult his legal department, his outside lawyers, his outside legal specialists. And in each case, a decision must be made. The decisions must encompass both the opinion of the legal specialist as to what may be done and the opinion of the businessman as to what degree of risk is justified. There is no black-and-white legal answer to most of the questions put to the lawyers. The answers are, very largely, a matter of opinion or interpretation. No ethical businessman will do something clearly against the law; but every businessman must evaluate his lawyers' interpretations and advice and then decide for himself what measure of risk is involved with proceeding. Since there is often no completely risk-free way, such evaluation can be a very difficult decision-making process.

It therefore provides the opportunities for extraordinary procrastination. "We'd better check legal?" is a phrase that every competent businessman *must* use regularly—but it is one that I have come to tremble at. It is, of course, the lawyer's job to advise one about risks and to keep one out of trouble. Unfortunately, the easiest way for an underachieving lawyer to do that is to say "No" to everything, and the easiest way for the underachieving businessman is then to do nothing. Since business contains only a few overachievers, the red tape of the law has become one of its worst snarls. Murray Bloom, in his book, *The Trouble with Lawyers,* quite unfairly castigates all lawyers and quotes an old gypsy curse: "May you have a lawsuit in which you know you are in the right." Fortunately, he grossly exaggerates. In the law as in business there are many tough, bright, sometimes brilliant lawyers who love achievement. George DeGenaro, a hard-skiing, feisty lawyer who is a partner in a major law firm and as such carries considerable influence with many clients, is typical of the best of lawyers: he rarely says "No." Instead, he says: "Here's how you can best do it and here's the risk." While there are many like him, there are always too few. I, like every businessman, wish there were more!

Behind this whole theme of law and procrastination lies a philosophic dilemma of today's business society. With business organizations aggrandizing power in accelerating degree, the major question is whether those same organizations should take over the social responsibility of creating law—some lawyers in business organizations believe that to be at least partly their job. They feel that since it is the law's purpose to protect the weaker partner in a contractual relationship from the stronger, and since, as corporate lawyers, they are frequently representative of the stronger, they should recognize the social point of view of the weaker. Obviously, however, there is a massive conflict of interest inherent in that point of view. No lawyer can be effective in representing both ends against the middle. Perhaps a representative of the people is required within a business organization; but if that is true, I believe he is needed in all major organizations, including consumer groups. As Peter Drucker writes in *The Age of Discontinuity:*

> *The ombudsman . . . is needed to champion the individ-ual against management in the business corporation, but also against the labor union, whatever the latter's claim to 'represent the workers.' He is needed in and against the government agency, but also in and against the university. The ombudsman is, so to speak, the hy-giene of organizations—or at least their toothbrush.*

But if the ombudsman is needed, he is not to be the corporate lawyer. In this Mr. Drucker and I could not be more completely in agreement.

When you get right down to it, the difference between George DeGenaro and his ilk and the run of procrastinating lawyers may not be only that one is an achiever and the other not—although, obviously, this is a major part of the difference. But it may also be that DeGenaro agrees that, in a corporate sense, his responsibility is to help the corporation do what it was created to do, while the procrastinating lawyer may feel that his responsibility includes trying to help the organization do "good" in areas in which it was not intended to operate at all. This general desire for "good" is, of course, consistent with a lack of desire for achievement: specific corporate objectives can be objectively measured as having been either achieved or not; but working to do "good" is so vague that its success or failure can never be proven at all.

Perhaps, however, all this thinking extends beyond the question of underachievement and legal procrastination. While it is true that the lawyer may indulge in procrastination for reasons of "social concern," it is much more true and far more frequent that he does so because, in the legal profession just as in every other profession, there are more under- than overachievers.

Consultants are another cause of potential procrastination. "Let's ask the advertising agency," or "What does McKinsey think?" (McKinsey & Co. being among the most prestigious of the management consulting firms), or "We'll check with our bankers," are all phrases that the overachiever in business uses but often learns to dread. Not that these types of institutions are of no value. On the contrary, they often provide the objective advice, the idea, and even the stimulation to action which is so vital. Unfortunately, it is the very fact that they *are* good that can sometimes make them into such effective causes of procrastination. The problem is that it is difficult for an outside consulting firm to consider a path being suggested by their client and say simply: "Yes, you are right. We quite agree." If they were to do that with any regularity, how could they justify their fees? Thus, it happens frequently that, except for the most elite and respected of consultants—those to whom total faith by the client is justified and given—consultants feel that they have no alternative but to respond to many questions with lengthy disagreements.

The same problem applies, of course, if the experts are not outside consultants but are permanently employed by the company itself.

Harry Jones's so-called executive job was as product manager in charge of a famous old washing detergent. The brand had been going steadily downhill for a number of years and required a complete reintroduction and revitalization to alter the path of its business. It was up to Harry to make the necessary changes in packaging, in promotion, and in advertising.

One of the experts whose job it was to pass on the suitability of the changes he wanted to make was the director of promotion coordination or some such title; he could not be circumvented. He was also a staff "expert" who felt that, for someone in his job, agreement was heretical. Inevitably he insisted upon making some "contribution"—usually a simple reversal of whatever the brand manager presented. If they showed him blue lettering on a red background, he would always ask for red on blue. Stubbornly, Harry Jones fought for his point of view, and lost every time. After all, the director, not Harry, was the expert. Finally Harry got smart. From then on he always presented precisely the opposite of what he wanted—and when the sales expert made his almost inevitable "suggestion," Harry simply and instantaneously reversed field!

Procrastinations are not intended to try the overachiever—nor to allow the underachiever in business, or even the normal, nonachieving, cautious executive, to delay decisions with impunity. But sometimes it seems that way. Fortunately, however, the overachiever, with his driving determination to get action, almost invariably overcomes the procrastinating techniques so that, in his hands, they are metamorphosed from procrastinations to aids. He uses market research forcefully to give him information he lacks. (In doing so, incidentally, he endears himself to most market research departments, which love productive research and hate to be used as a tactic of delay.) He obtains from the lawyers sound answers because he asks action-oriented questions. He says: "I'm going to move this ball forward. What precautions do you recommend to minimize the risks?" not, "Is it okay to move it?" He says: "Show me how to make this commercial acceptable to the governmental authorities" not, "Will you approve this commercial?" In doing so, he manages to move forward. And with him moves industry.

How Overachievers
Build Businesses

It is a sad but true fact that most men cannot get anything done. They are full of explanations, full of excuses, full of justifications and rationalizations. But action is lacking. In the business world, such men may be administratively competent in the sense that they handle satisfactorily the great load of paper work generated each day whether or not the business is moving forward. Or, as in the case of one chief executive whose company almost went bankrupt before his bankers finally managed to sell it for him, they may write tomes of justifiable complaints and valuable directions only to wait in vain for their staff to act upon them.

Michael was an experienced group product manager in charge of four of his company's most important brands with aggregate sales of well over $50 million. He was reputed to be a first-class man, slated for advancement. He was also a delightful chap, thoroughly informed, and apparently full of initiative. But when a new marketing vice president joined the company, he noticed, over the first few weeks, that none of the projects Michael had told him about seemed to be moving forward. One of them, about which Mike had expressed great enthusiasm, was his idea of bringing out a line of men's toiletries under the name of a world-famous New York restaurant. He felt that such a line, merchandised initially to the restaurant's large mailing list, would have the right sort of prestige and glamour. The new marketing chief agreed and wanted to know how the negotiations were going.

To his surprise Mike told him that he had not actually talked to the restaurant company. "Previous management [by which the v.p. assumed he meant anyone but himself] turned it down," Mike said. "They didn't like the idea."

"Why not?"

Michael was at a complete loss for an answer. But the real payoff was that he didn't even know who had disapproved!

Of course, the new v.p. encouraged him to proceed. Nevertheless, two years later that project had still not moved forward. Certainly Mike had talked to the restaurant. Certainly, they were interested. But no action resulted. Neither success nor failure. Nothing. Worse, during those two years there was not a single instance in which Michael initiated anything at all. His brands, his product managers, his department, everything was always in perfect shape: the sort of perfect shape that it is possible to achieve only when standing absolutely still. In the meantime, of course, the rest of the company rushed forward and, slowly and inevitably, Michael's department became less and less important. Eventually, it was merged with another and Michael was asked to leave the company.

My father is president of a company that has had a remarkable string of successes. It is a small but highly respected firm with a justified reputation for creating successful, profitable products. A short while ago he offered a new decongestant system to one of the larger makers of nasal decongestants. The new system works very much the same way as the old vaporizer decongestant system that they now sell; but it works dry rather than in water, and therefore requires no expensive electric appliance to evaporate the water. Moreover, it is a very cheap product to manufacture and would have a low consumer price even if a substantial profit were built in for the manufacturer. It is thoroughly patent-protected so that there would be very little danger of a competitor rapidly copying the product. On the face of it, my father's new product is almost essential to the company to whom he offered it.

To my surprise, however, the president of the company responded politely but firmly, "No, thank you." By way of minimal explanation he added: "Your product would seem to be substantially better than ours and would, therefore, tend to cannibalize our present business. We would not be interested in bringing out a new product which could replace sales of our existing product."

My father, who had predicted the rejection and was not surprised, was nevertheless saddened. "When I first did business with them, that man used to be such a driving force," he explained. "But the whole outfit now lacks sufficient creative stimulus and the poor chap has lost all the drive he used to have. In fact, the whole company has become bogged down in a morass of indecisiveness. It is the Peter Principle applied to a whole organization."

Inevitably, of course, another company will pick up the new decongestant and market it—and doubtless gobble up the "poor chap's" business, just as he himself predicted.

There are men who, even though they may not be strong enough to restart the dead motor of a stagnated company or to create a new business from nothing but guts and air, are nevertheless able to maintain and sometimes to accelerate the growth of an already moving company. These are the men who make up the large majority of successful middle and upper management. They are vital to the success of business and therefore of the nation. They are the men who can and must be trained to be at least reasonably effective, for there simply are not enough real achievers to go around. Drucker writes:

> If effectiveness were a gift people were born with, the way they are born with a gift for music or an eye for painting, we would be in bad shape, for we know that only a small minority is born with great gifts in any one of these areas. We would, therefore, be reduced to trying to spot people with high potential of effectiveness early and to train as best we know to develop their talent. But we could hardly hope to find enough people for the executive tasks of modern society this way.

I completely agree, although I suspect that, in writing for the mass of middle-management people, he has failed to recognize that it will always take those few extraordinary activists who are born with "great gifts" in effectiveness to start things. These rare men, whom I have designated the overachievers, will always be essential to provide the motive power for the ordinary men who can be trained to a reasonable level of effectiveness but who cannot be taught how to create movement where there is none. The overachiever vitally needs competent but ordinary men. There are so many more of them than of him; without them he can hardly hope to create the movement he craves.

By being in the right place at the right time—and by being trained in effectiveness as far as possible—these ordinary men participate in the apparently inevitable annual growth of their companies; and, as the just fruits of their success, gather to themselves prestige, pensions, and perhaps paunches. These are the men who seldom make the mistakes that sometimes overtake their more original and driving peers. At the end of their careers, they can look back on a life of achievement—provided they have remained reasonably lucky. They are not overachievers, but they are valuable men and not wasters of time. On the other hand, they may be quickly destroyed if things go wrong. Indeed, they are usually destroyed by any major change, right or wrong, for they lack the imagination and the resiliency to withstand major business or sociological shifts. They are the men who, although bright, well educated, trained in administration and effectiveness, and often beautifully mannered, not infrequently come abysmal croppers in the business world.

Some years ago a bright young manager was sent to a Latin American country to reorganize the subsidiary of a major American corporation. The subsidiary was close to bankruptcy. The previous manager had been dishonest and libertine. He had introduced dozens of unsuccessful new products which remained, unsold and unsalable, in the retail trade. In a sense he was an overachiever: with vigor and flair he had rapidly achieved a major catastrophe!

The young manager moved into this disastrous situation with energy. He fired the sales manager for stealing; he borrowed money at half the earlier rates—but not from the previous president's moneylender friends; he eliminated the decorative young ladies who staffed a dozen sinecures; he cleared out the moldering products from the retail trade; he introduced several of the parent corporation's standard international products with a standard degree of success; he sold a large piece of real estate which, as it turned out, was partly owned by the president's cousin; and, within two or three years, he had the business reasonably profitable and holding its own. In the process he earned many accolades.

Five years later, however, the situation was quite different. During that time the country, which had earlier been going through a series of political and military upheavals, first stabilized and then started growing dynamically. All business boomed. Corporations grew at annual rates of 25 percent as a norm. And the young manager's own company, settled now, well staffed, conservatively financed, with some sound products in the market place and good trade relations, sat poised on the edge of tremendous expansion opportunities and unheard of profitability. But the careful young manager remembered how his conservatism had been praised. He recalled how his predecessor's penchant for introducing new products had resulted in disaster. So instead of seizing the opportunity for growth, he continued to do what he had been trained to do and congratulated for doing, namely, to keep his firm's fires carefully damped. He did not realize that the band wagon had changed direction.

As a result, and to his total surprise, he, in his turn, was asked to resign.

If most men can achieve relatively little, and only a small group of highly trained managers can show even the effectiveness of continuing to do well what is already being done, then the real overachievers must be rare indeed. They are those few men who leave a monument of achievement. One way to characterize them is to say that they are the men who do the things which would never have been done without them.

The most famous overachievers, Helena Rubinstein, for example, who built the cosmetic empire carrying her name, or Ross Perault, who built a $200-million fortune in five years in the electronics business—and then tried unsuccessfully to take over Wall Street—or Leonard Lavin, who built Alberto Culver from scratch in direct competition with such enormously powerful companies as Colgate–Palmolive, Procter and Gamble and Bristol–Meyers, become famous, almost household words. These are geniuses of achievement. They are the exceptions because they have the drive for overachievement coupled with enormous acumen and devilish luck. But what of other men, mere "mortal" men, who have the drive to overachieve but who have no more than normal intelligence and ability? The fact is that they succeed too. They too leave landmarks. They too get something done.

Jack Landry created the Marlboro brand of cigarettes for Philip Morris. He *was* the Marlboro man. His friendship with Pete Rozelle, the Commissioner of the National Football League, dates back to the days when every football player endorsed Marlboro as, it seemed, did every athlete in every other field, as did every virile giant who ever lunched at Toots Shor's restaurant. It was the success of Marlboro, today battling for first place in cigarette sales, that allowed Philip Morris to grow from a substantial company into the giant it is today, involved in everything from mass housing to paper production.

One of the traditional ways in which overachievers, great and small, have sought to create action is to leave the confines of big business and seek to move forward as private entrepreneurs. In today's environment this is frequently a less successful means of achieving action than it seems at first sight. Usually, big business is so much better equipped to move forward that even the "moment of inertia" found in large organizations is less inhibiting than is the lack of strength, power, and money the entrepreneur faces alone. Nevertheless, the adventure and putative freedom of starting his own business frequently starts to fascinate the overachiever. Being the type of man he is, he then moves forward along this path with just as much determination as he showed in trying to create action within big business.

The most important problem he has to solve is how to find enough money.

The best way, of course, is if he or his family is rich. But if this is not the case, he has to go to Wall Street—or its equivalent in other cities—and find venture capitalists willing to back him.

Raising money on Wall Street is an enormously difficult and time-consuming activity. Essentially, it is nonproductive in the sense that it is the prerequisite to achievement, but not achievement in itself.

A successful young marketing man I shall call Wendell James broke his leg rather badly one hot summer and found himself lying in a hospital bed wired over a series of pulleys in miserable immobility.

As he lay there, bored and downcast, a friend called Harry, one of the slower talking, faster thinking men in New York, came to visit him, apparently with no other motive than to wish him well. Harry is a private entrepreneur, an administrator and promoter. He works alone, putting things together and taking them apart—but always ending up with a piece for himself.

"How does one raise money, Harry?" Wendell James asked.

"With difficulty!" And then after a pause, "Wall Street, if you're lucky."

"Do you know anyone there?" It was a rhetorical question: Harry knows someone absolutely everywhere. Most places seem to be populated entirely by his relatives.

"What sort of anyone?" he asked.

They talked a little longer and Harry promised to introduce Wendell to an appropriate friend of his "sometime."

When Harry smells a profit opportunity which involves little effort on his part, "sometime" generally means sooner than you think. Nevertheless, Wendell was surprised when the very next day the door opened and in came Harry, pulling behind him a somewhat reluctant major figure in an important investment banking house on Wall Street. You must picture the scene. Wendell lay there, still immobilized in traction. His bed was rumpled; the weather was hot so he had discarded his pajama top and pushed down the bedclothes until he was three-quarters naked; and, having just awoken from somewhat drugged sleep, his face was puffy and his hair tousled.

"Let me introduce Wendell James to you," said Harry, turning to his friend. "He is one of the most dynamic businessmen in America today!"

That was the first step in the founding of Wendell's first company. It was a somewhat unsteady slipway down which to launch a new entrepreneur. But Wendell James says that he has never regretted one moment.

Obviously, however, there is a great deal more to the founding of a company than just contacts. In almost every case the speculative investor looks for a combination of: an idea—the more exciting the better—that gives the potential new venture a reasonable chance of dramatic growth and profit improvement; something solid which, he hopes, will be leavened and expanded to glory by the shining idea, but which in the mean-time provides a sensible, safe investment base; and a manager or, preferably, a group of managers capable of running the solid company effectively and of implementing the new idea brilliantly. Exactly the same requirements exist for a new venture within a large company. Top management always asks the same questions: Can we see a chance of touching the stars? Can we limit our risk? Have we the people to pull it off?

In this context, let us examine the founding of a typical company. It was the brain child and achievement of the same Wendell James, fully recovered and very much on the move. I have changed the name of the company and its field of business in order to protect confidentiality. But in all other respects the facts are correct.

The company, Special Foods, Inc., was started by Wendell in 1965.

At the start was a simple idea made plausible because its effectiveness had been demonstrated in other industries. The idea was to apply sound principles of modern mass marketing, by which virtually all major marketing companies have grown, to the specialty foods industry, where such marketing had been practically unknown. Marketing has been used, refined, improved, and relied upon for decades by practically every company selling heavily through supermarkets or drug stores. Colgate–Palmolive, as well as Procter and Gamble and Lever Bros., live from marketing. General Foods, Consolidated Foods, Beatrice Foods, Hunt Foods, and even Hershey Foods use marketing techniques as a daily activity. Great advertising agencies (even the new "creative" ones) survive on marketing. And marketing consultants multiply as fast as CIA agents in an emerging nation! But at that time the specialty foods business had not yet felt the impact of Chun King or gourmet frozen foods. Marketing had largely passed it by.

First, to be clear what I am talking about, let me define what I mean by marketing. As I use the term, it means simply the *science* and *art* of persuading the consumer to try and then consistently use a product.

The *science* of marketing is crucial; but it is almost totally limited to the development of a product that, in at least one significant way, is superior to any other product on the market.

Virtually all the great marketing successes have, at their beginning, a genuine product advantage. The Volkswagen automobile was a success not primarily because the brilliant advertising created by Doyle Dane Bernbach popularized "The Bug" throughout the country, but because The Bug was an extraordinary little piece of mechanical achievement. Ivory Soap was successful not mainly because of the famous phrases "99 and 44/100% Pure," "It floats," but rather because it was the first wholly consistent, pure soap and, by golly, it *did* float! Colgate toothpaste, Contac, Tampax, nylon, M&M's candy, Benson & Hedges 100's, Helena Rubinstein's brush-on-peel-off mask, the explosion of cranberry-based products, Formica, and many, many others were, at their outset, better products. Sometimes the product was lower in price; a good product which costs less than others like it is, of course, in one respect, a "better" product. All new and better products were rapidly imitated, but few of the imitators, if they had no technical advantages of their own, were as successful commercially as the original, technically advanced product.

Similarly, most major marketing failures—and obviously they are often hard to remember—were not so much the result of improper marketing as of ill-conceived or poor products: there was too little science in them. The Edsel was a disaster because nobody liked the car, not because the advertising was poor. Shasta Hair Shampoo had nothing to offer as a new product. And do you remember the brief splurge of chlorophyll toothpastes? They died as soon as people realized that the products didn't deliver their promises—or any promises! Burma-Shave, for all its fantastically popular road signs, never had a superior product and never achieved strong sales. What ever happened to Vote toothpaste; soap-impregnated dish cloths; Bugles, Whistles, and Daisies snacks; Morris Minor cars (which exist in the United States but hardly compare to the number of Japanese cars, although they abound in England where they are protected by tariff barriers); most of the quick food franchises; Tressy dolls, which made a brief but abortive attack on the highly successful Barbie doll; and some hundreds of dreadfully overpriced and overrated men's toiletries? All of them fell by the wayside not because they lacked marketing art (although some lacked even this) but because there was no new product idea, no product science involved.

The *art* of marketing is not, however, to be taken as unimportant. There will always be examples of products that are technically sound, although not extraordinary, but which fail because they do not come clearly and attractively to the attention of the consuming public. Similarly, there are many examples of products that are only marginally superior to ones already in existence but which nevertheless achieve considerable success because of marketing art. Pepsi-Cola, for example, a "me too" product if ever there was one, has successfully attacked the originator of the idea, Coca Cola. It has grown to almost the size of its sire by seeming to be brighter, more vivacious, more "with it." Its up-beat advertising has become its distinguishing feature —its differentiation from Coke. As a result, Pepsi has become almost but still not quite as successful as Coca Cola, although in this case "almost" is very successful indeed.

The art of marketing, then, can be summarized as that art that allows the manufacturer to describe his product's technical point of advantage in a way particularly appealing to the consumer and then to disseminate that description in every possible way. The product's description is to be used in packaging, in in-store merchandising and, of course, in the formal advertising media.

In the specialty foods business of 1965, few people advertised. Those who did used generic statements: "delicious," "good to eat," etc. Even in the related candy industry, the largest advertiser used "indescribably delicious" as its advertising message. There is nothing preemptive about that claim, nor is it specifically descriptive. Allowing for a certain amount of advertising "puffery," anyone can claim that his product is "indescribably delicious." The phrase is certainly no more applicable to Peter Paul Mounds or Almond Joy than it is to Hershey's Chocolate bars or, indeed, to pizza, cereals, or steak.

Not only was effective advertising rare in the specialty foods industry, but even where it did exist it was almost never carried through to package design, in-store merchandising, public relations releases, and so on.

It was this idea of applying the "art of marketing" to the specialty foods industry that lay at the heart of the original creation of Special Foods, Inc. It was a strong idea and it provided the first of the three requirements for a new business venture. It was sufficient to interest a number of key backers in a new company that would acquire several specialty foods businesses, weld them together into one major "food agglomerate," and apply the proven principles of modern marketing to the resultant new company to make it more successful than the sum of its parts. Laboriously (for there is no other way) Wendell put together the business document, the blueprint for the new venture.

The second step, probably the most vital step for the investors, was to add "security" to the "idea." This meant acquiring solidly established companies with machinery and equipment, bricks and mortar, and a sound reputation for making good products (goodwill), which would provide intrinsic values unlikely to evaporate. In this way, even if the "idea" proved unsound, the investors could feel reasonably protected against a major loss on the deal. (I should add parenthetically that, in my opinion, this feeling of safety which investors crave and usually demand is almost always an illusion. There is little safety in buying any business but less if the business is small. Few owners of such enterprises are willing to sell for a reasonable price unless they foresee some real problems for their business—problems the buyer cannot anticipate.)

The moment Wendell first saw the company his backers wanted to acquire, his heart sank. It was a rambling agglomeration of five buildings, dingy and full of aging machinery. For the first time he realized what too few financial men ever learn: that a good balance sheet and a happy-looking profit-and-loss record can hide a multitude of problems; yes, and in some cases, a multitude of sins! He tried desperately to explain to his backers that his idea would come to life faster and be better if it was not encumbered by any old and probably moribund business. He recommended strongly against any acquisition and argued that they start from scratch. But the more he talked, the more he realized that acquisitions were going to be necessary. Ideas alone are simply not financeable. Finally, even though he realized that it would take him some time to modernize the company and implement his marketing techniques, he agreed to make the acquisition—at least it was better than anything else available.

Instantly, he faced a million problems. They seemed to tumble in on one another so fast that they blurred. The fact that sleep became a luxury to which he could devote little time may have contributed to the blur.

All of which underlines the fact that getting things started is easier than keeping them going. Where a new and vigorous motive force is suddenly superimposed on a static or slowly declining situation there is bound to be the devil to pay. It is then, as Wendell found, that days run into nights and both run into weeks and your friends ask why they never see you any more and you fall asleep while you are trying to explain.

That is when you need the third of the key requirements for which investment bankers—or corporation managers—look: a strong management team.

Wendell was fortunate in having just such a team. It consisted of a marketing man, a production man, and a financial man. They were the three vice presidents who, with Wendell, founded and ran the company. They were zealous movers and achievers with their cutting edges honed.

Within months, they had made three further acquisitions and pulled the wavering companies they bought into one growing entity. They were on the verge of success.

Unfortunately, just as things were looking good, the financiers who were backing Wendell James decided that they could afford no further investment —or perhaps they felt that they no longer needed the tough and rather opinionated founder. In any case, they withheld funds and soon Special Foods, without enough cash or working capital, was teetering on the edge of disaster.

After several months of growing problems and growing mistrust between Wendell and his tight group of employees and the bankers, Wendell was forced out. Just three years after he had founded the company he left its helm. Shortly thereafter, by mutual agreement, his friends and co-founders left too.

On the day of his departure, he made a speech to all the employees thanking them, wishing them well for the future, and asking them to be as loyal to his successor as they had been to him. He was convinced that the business was solid. His successor was a first-class executive with a sound administrative record. The company's products were good, correctly priced, and well marketed. The factories were running smoothly. What could go wrong? He was sure that the company would continue to improve and would make money. He even purchased more stock on the open market after he left. It was the worst investment he ever made!

What happened was totally different from what he or anyone else expected. Instead of continuing to grow, the company first leveled off and then started to slide. Soon it started to miss its monthly sales objective. Inevitably, it was forced to cut its advertising, thus suffering more.

Worse, it took only a few weeks before the sales organization lost its enthusiasm and before manufacturing efficiency started to fall. Then the accounting and administrative departments, which had always been terribly understaffed because of lack of money, and had been held together by hard work and sealing wax, started to fall apart. Shipments were misplaced and customer complaints ignored.

Finally, the suppliers, sensing that the company was moribund, refused to extend further credit—and the end was near. By late 1970, about two years after Wendell James left, Special Foods, Inc., was forced into reorganization under Chapter 11 of the bankruptcy act.

It took only two years—approximately the same length of time that it had taken to build it from zero to $30 million of sales—for it to decline to a sales level of under $10 million and file for reorganization.

And yet, as I look from the outside into the two years of the company's decline, I can see very little that was actually done differently from that done during the years of its growth. The procedures that Wendell's team of overachievers had established were kept, largely unaltered. The sales organization that had worked so well under him was left, largely unchanged. The marketing patterns he had set up continued to be used. There seemed to be no basically wrong decisions made. Yet the company stopped progressing.

I believe that the reason is clear: the replacement of the founding achievers by standard administrators came too early in the history of the corporation, before it had enough momentum to continue to coast under its own weight. "The small man runs hard because the bet is all or nothing," writes Robert Heller in *The Great Executive Dream*. When Wendell started, he and his men were certainly running hard. But after they left, there was no incentive to run so hard. Instead there were fine executives who administered the company as effectively as if it were some strong and well-established concern, conservatively, procedurally. But they were the sort of men who did not want to expose themselves or their families to financial risk. They were ever conscious that they would always find secure employment in some other commercial bureaucracy provided they made no *definable* mistakes at Special Foods, Inc. There was too much emphasis on the team and not enough on forcing action from the top. Usually, total reliance by a chief on "the team" suggests that, individually, the players are not very effective.

I believe that no achiever can really inherit the work of another and expect to continue it without losing momentum. In this case, it was too early in the company's life for it to withstand any such deceleration.

In *Management and Machiavelli,* Antony Jay writes that a "characteristic shared by successful generals and successful industrial leaders is the urge to get the initiative." It may well be that in the absence of the entrepreneurs like Wendell James and his founding colleagues at Special Foods, Inc., the second generation of management in any new company is always in danger of losing the initiative to its competition. Once the initiative is lost and achievement stops, the company will almost immediately cease to function successfully. Then, unless the company is mature enough to survive on its own momentum, its only hope is that some new overachiever will emerge in time to save it.

7

The Overachiever
and Change

The first thing to understand in order to study the question of how the overachiever promotes change within existing major business organizations is why such organizations often appear to be set against change when, at the same time, they frequently recognize its value and even seek to encourage it. Why is the effort needed to overcome their inertia often so much greater than that needed to keep them moving in whatever direction they happen to be moving—even if that direction is wrong?

The answer is so obvious as to seem almost puerile; the obvious is often simplistic. The simple fact here is that, in order to arrange for many thousands of people to move toward any one or even any limited number of objectives, it is necessary to dictate clear-cut guidelines for everyone—and insist on no deviation. If you consider how difficult it is to get five people together for dinner at a given restaurant at a given time on a given day—surely no overwhelming feat of logistics—you begin to have some inkling of how inordinately difficult it must be to arrange for ten thousand men and women to work toward the same complex objectives. That is why management insists on a "procedure book." That is why conformity is rewarded and innovation often appears to be opposed. Confucius would have been an excellent business administrator. "Keep order among them by ritual and they will come to you of their own accord," he said. And business operates by the ritual of procedures.

Even in the most decentralized business, where several specific objectives may be set, one for each decentralized division, it is necessary to have some over-all set of rules. Without such rules it would become enormously difficult for the divisions to work together toward one corporate goal.

Since the body of rules needed becomes more complex as the organization becomes larger, it is quite clear that very large organizations, with so many rules that they are hardly assimilable, require in addition to the factual procedures a sort of over-all corporate attitude, a corporate feeling of how to think, a corporate "religion." Jay, in *Management and Machiavelli*, has written about this idea in some detail. "A corporation, like a state, needs a faith," he says. He is thinking primarily in terms of keeping the employees happy, but I would add that it requires that faith also to make sure that all the employees tend to think about problems and their solutions in a comparable way. Only in this manner can the corporation be sure that when a new problem arises, one not envisaged in the procedure book, all employees who come in contact with it will tend to resolve it in a similar way and, above all, in a way not antithetical to the aims of the corporation as a whole. Writes Marshall McLuhan, "Every corporation needs a noble ideal . . . it also fights *deviants.* This faith is based on the assumptions upon which their success was founded—their experience."

I would go so far as to suggest that one of the main reasons for committees in business—since they are hardly famous for their ability to get anything done—is to explain and reinforce the over-all religion of the organization. Just as church religions tend to drum in their faith through meetings, services, and the repetition of creeds, so, I believe, committees are vital to the perpetuation of the creeds in businesses. At its lowest level, the committee is a sales meeting; and there can be no doubt that the purpose of the sales meeting is far more to provide an understanding of the corporate religion than to provide specific information.

If you have any doubts about the importance of an established religion for major business organizations, attend any twenty-five-year pin ceremony or any ceremony connected with the retirement of an old employee. The words used, the attitudes taken, even the faces of the participants are those otherwise reserved for church!

Businesses founded and run by an autocratic tyrant who *is* the corporate religion frequently run into difficulties when the founder eventually leaves. It is possible, then, to maintain or renew the momentum of the business only by systematizing the direction, the religion the founder has personified.

The story of Madame Helena Rubinstein and the cosmetics company she founded and built into an international giant is a classic example of a personality and a company which first prospered mightily and then almost floundered, first as a result of the leadership and then of the death of its founder. Indeed, the whole cosmetics industry is full of companies built by glamorous, larger-than-life entrepreneurs that suffered grievously when those entrepreneurs were forced to leave the helm.

In 1973, Colgate–Palmolive acquired the Helena Rubinstein Company, and I became associated with Rubinstein shortly thereafter. The company was typical of those which suffered when their founding overachiever died. I believe, therefore, that the story of how Rubinstein's management has systematized the mystique of Madame Rubinstein and thus turned a declining business around is instructive. I shall describe it in some detail:

The great old cosmetic houses, Helena Rubinstein, Elizabeth Arden, Max Factor—their very names evoke nostalgia for the opulence of the twenties in Paris, Boston and Hollywood—were founded by tough overachievers whose drive for action led them to an imperial, idiosyncratic, dramatic, flamboyant, and tyrannical leadership that plunged their companies forward throughout this century on the crest of America's great wave of economic growth. The more recent cosmetic tycoons, Charles Revson of Revlon, Estée Lauder, and even more recently, Polly Bergen or Mary Quant, are similarly dynamic, colorful, occasionally eccentric people. All of them have had that sense of showmanship normally associated with the moguls who founded Hollywood motion-picture companies; all were individualists who wielded their power with iron fists—however scented the knuckles and polished the nails.

This mode of leadership, while it built these early cosmetics enterprises into major businesses, was not conducive to efficient management. Once the ebullient founders dropped out, leaving large but disorderly empires behind, it was inevitable that, to survive, their companies would have to be acquired by larger, better-organized and -financed corporations. In addition to Helena Rubinstein being owned by Colgate–Palmolive, Elizabeth Arden is today owned by Lilly; Coty by Pfizer; Lanvin/Charles of the Ritz by Squibb; Max Factor by Norton Simon; Germaine Monteille, Yardley, and others by British–American Tobacco; and Dorothy Gray and others by Sterling Drug. These acquisitions have not been unmitigated successes. Attempts to replace the "management by mystique" of the founders with conventional management techniques have frequently not been rewarding. Among the earlier acquisitions, Elizabeth Arden ran at a loss in 1972 of $2.5 million on sales of $76.0 million. Coty, purchased by the Pfizer Company in 1962, is said still to be financially unsatisfactory. Dorothy Gray has not prospered under Sterling Drug. And Gillette, which made a brief sortie into the cosmetic business by acquiring Eve of Roma, turned tail and ran when it realized the difficulties it was getting into. The more recent acquisitions may be in somewhat less trouble. A 1971 acquisition of Lanvin/Charles of the Ritz by Squibb faces problems but continues to be profitable, and Kirk Parrish, the president installed by Squibb, feels confident that the business can be built. The acquisition of Max Factor for some $418 million by the Norton Simon conglomerate in 1973 may also turn out to be successful. In the year of acquisition, Max Factor's earnings contributed $36 million or over 25 percent of Norton Simon's total profits. On the other hand, the earlier acquisitions, too, seemed initially successful. It remains to be seen whether the more recent ones will set a new pattern by continuing to show success. The jury is still out, and the problems are immense.

The essence of the problems is always the same: how is it possible to replace the "management by mystique," which was the hallmark of the founding entrepreneurs, by big-business management? As Emerson pointed out, "every natural power exhilarates," and the founders of the great cosmetic empires were "natural powers" indeed. When they died or retired, the exhilaration died with them. After a time, the organizations they left behind inevitably started to decline. For cosmetics are both technology and dream. Many of the good treatment creams that women use to improve the quality of their skin are truly effective in the sense that regular use will give softer, smoother, better-looking skin than irregular use or none. But they are obviously not wholly effective; a woman of eighty *always* looks older than a woman of twenty. Moreover, a single application of any treatment product does not solve the problem of wrinkles or sagging skin; it helps but does not cure. Color products, such as lipstick and eye shadow are, of course, totally effective in the sense that they do impart color as desired. But effective at what? The woman judges effectiveness of color products not by whether they color, but by whether they make her look the way she wants to look. Here too, no cosmetic can be wholly effective on most women. In order for a woman to accept as efficacious her treatment cream or as attractive her color make-up, she has to *believe* in it. It is an act of faith for the woman to believe that she looks as young and beautiful as is possible.

This faith has been strengthened because, in almost every case, cosmetics have been endorsed by a glamorous, larger-than-life, promotional genius whose example it was easy to follow and to believe in.

Madame Helena Rubinstein, Princess Gourielli, was such a figure. When she advertised that her cream made women look younger, they believed her. It was a pattern of didacticism that she followed all her life. When she first arrived in Australia, already, as the *Cleveland Plain Dealer* would describe her twenty years later, a "character of incredible chutzpah, a woman so maddening yet so remarkable that she was—and is—unforgettable," she had in her luggage twelve bottles of Cream Valaze. And when she announced to the women of Australia that cosmetics must treat as well as beautify their skin, she faced (and brooked) no argument. It became the basic premise on which she founded a business which was to grow into a world-wide, highly profitable cosmetic company and which was to allow her, in her later years, to live in the opulent style of a Marie Antoinette and wield the "whim of iron" of a Queen Victoria. She ran her life and her business exactly as she pleased. *The Saturday Review* said of a biography about her, called *Madame,* that it re-created "the human whirlwind Helena Rubinstein generated wherever she went . . . the parties . . . [were] grand affairs—as . . . [were] the personalities . . . she was one of a kind."

In business she operated by inspired instinct. She may have described those jars of Cream Valaze in her book *My Life for Beauty* as "the finger of fate," but they represented a new type of product and a new idea. Doubtless they were as well thought out as were her later inventions.

She knew what she liked; and what she didn't she swept from her desk into an untidy, rejected heap on the floor. She played her executives off against one another, fostering their jealousies rather than trying to create a team spirit. She was brilliant but erratic. She moved forward by feeling, not by plan; but move forward she did, with constant, determined momentum. When she died in 1965 at the age of ninety-four she left a dynamic company full of new ideas, but lacking, as she herself was lacking, in orderliness and in careful, modern, business organization.

As a result, from that day until 1973, when the Helena Rubinstein Company was acquired by Colgate–Palmolive, her empire slowly lost momentum; without her drive there was no plan. By 1972, the year before Colgate acquired the company, over-all profits had fallen to $1,754,000 and the American company, the heart of the whole organization, made a loss of $4,225,000. No person and no system had been able to replace Madame Rubinstein's genius.

Starting in late 1973, the Helena Rubinstein Company reestablished its lost business momentum by creating or, more correctly, recreating a "corporate religion" with Madame Rubinstein in the deity role. There is mounting evidence that this approach is achieving success.

The new grand corporate strategy was to reestablish and emphasize what Madame Rubinstein stood for (or should have stood for), and then break down this idealized image into a specific seven-point program designed to systematize the "Mystique of Madame Rubinstein." These seven principles were:

1. The "Science of Beauty"

Madame Rubinstein's basic idea was that cosmetic products, whether strictly color products like lipsticks, noncolor products like creams, cleansers, and toners, or slightly colored products like powders, must all improve the quality, that is the softness, smoothness, and general appearance of the skin. She believed that to achieve this objective it was necessary to enlist the aid of science in the search for beauty. As indicated by a broad market research study conducted in late 1973, the image of the Helena Rubinstein Company in consumers' minds still reflected this view. Consumers believe in Madame Rubinstein: the image of the company today remains what, for seventy years, Madame Rubinstein said it was.

This basic concept was christened "The Science of Beauty." Every advertisement run by the company is now under the heading, "The Science of Beauty," and so is every piece of display material and every press release.

Equally important, the influence of this "Science of Beauty" concept accounts for the new dynamism in the development of new products in the research and development laboratories. It accounts also for an entire new program of consumer education, including more authoritative and informative package directions, in-store leaflets, beauty hints, more informative (and less "precious") advertising copy, and even in-store promotions that teach consumers how to use Rubinstein products.

The "Science of Beauty" has resulted in increasing emphasis being placed on training schools for in-store beauty consultants; it has also resulted in a program to acquire patents for new types of products. For example, Skin Dew's Visible Action Day and Night Creams combine a normal moisturizing cream with "isolates" of the active milk protein ingredient in such a way that, although the ingredient and the cream are entirely miscible—and do mix when they reach the skin—they are kept discrete and unmixed in the jar or tube.

When the "Science of Beauty" was originally unveiled it was done through a presentation to the press in which Dr. Jack Mausner, the head of research and development for Helena Rubinstein, and Mala Rubinstein, the very figurehead of fashion both in the company and in the industry, shared the honors and together dramatized how science and beauty work together in Helena Rubinstein to create an integrated "Science of Beauty" company. Madame (at least as the company now envisages her) would have done the same thing.

2. A Specific Consumer: The "Real Woman"

Madame Rubinstein knew the consumer to whom she was directing her products, and had her image clearly in her mind. After her, however, the type of woman who was to be the Helena Rubinstein customer was no longer clear. Some company executives felt she should be the ordinary suburban housewife; others felt she should be the international socialite.

In late 1973 the broad market research studies the company had conducted were augmented and analyzed. As a result it became possible to break all cosmetic-using women into six basic categories and decide which was the right target audience for the company's products. The six groups were:

a. Ten percent of women were totally uninterested in cosmetics, and even in their personal appearance. They tended to be unkempt and dirty. Their houses, and frequently their minds, seemed to be littered with debris. They were nicknamed "The Slobs." Quite obviously they were not a Helena Rubinstein target audience.

b. The second group, which was named "The Worker Bees," were light cosmetic users. About 10 percent of women fell into this category. They were hard-working and dedicated, sometimes fanatically so; frequently they were professionals in such fields as social work. In whatever profession they found themselves, they were not interested in their appearance, provided it was clean and tidy. Their use of cosmetics tended to be limited to a few simple treatment creams. Even though they were likely to use Rubinstein products in this respect, they were clearly not a prime target audience for the company's marketing efforts.

c. The third group accounted for 25 percent of the population. It was given the name of "The Girl Next Door" group because it consisted of women who were interested primarily in household and children. They tended to be dependent and strongly influenced by their husbands' views; they wanted to do what was "normal." In cosmetic use they followed a conservative distance behind the leaders of fashion, and such use tended to be limited to special occasions. This was a group which Helena Rubinstein found an interesting potential audience—but it was not the prime target.

d. At the other end of the spectrum was the outgoing, somewhat wild woman —promptly dubbed "The Kook"—who tended toward only the latest fads: silver nail polish, green frosted hair, golden beauty marks. She accounted for approximately 10 percent of the population, and was clearly not a Helena Rubinstein potential customer.

e. The group closest to the "kook" was the highly fashionable, frequently wealthy woman who led fashion trends and used a great deal of cosmetics. Her nickname became "The Fashion Model." She accounted for approximately 20 percent of the population and was a high-potential cosmetic user. She was more interested, however, in color than in treatment. On balance, while she was an excellent Helena Rubinstein prospect, she was probably not right at the center of the company's target audience. Later, a check between this type and the type of consumer who rated Helena Rubinstein as among her most popular brands indicated that, while there was a positive correlation, Rubinstein did not do as well among "fashion model" types as did certain other companies.

f. Between "The Girl Next Door" and "The Fashion Model" lay one further category accounting for a total of 25 percent of all women. These were self-assured, understated, up-to-date women who were interested in "being in fashion," but not in leading it. They wanted their appearance to be dignified at all times, and were determined to make the best of their skin, and indeed of all aspects of themselves. They used cosmetics virtually every day and they used more skin treatment products than any other group.

These women fit exactly into the Helena Rubinstein image. A cross check with other data indicated that the reputation of the company among this group was better than among any other group. We called the type, rather self-servingly, "The Real Woman."

The image of the Helena Rubinstein customer, "The Real Woman," was established by this research. It is now completely understood, and "felt" as much as it was when Madame was alive. It has become part of the company's systematized mystique.

3. *Parameters of Taste—"Fashion White"*

Madame Rubinstein knew exactly what she liked and what she didn't. If she didn't like something, her eyes would blaze, her arms would flay about, she would knock over the articles being presented to her and berate everyone in sight. "Trash, *billig,*" she would repeat, "ridiculous, *dreck!*" Since she approved virtually everything created by the company, it followed that there was a pattern, a similarity, in everything the company developed. When she died this over-all image was lost. Every new man with any authority approved what he liked personally; but there was little similarity among their likes. It was necessary, therefore, to establish some parameters of taste which could reasonably continue to exist within a business organization staffed by a variety of paid managers whose personal tastes inevitably would vary. "Tell me what you like, and I'll tell you what you are," said John Ruskin; it was necessary for all Rubinstein executives to *like* the same thing for the company so that the company would always *be* the same thing.

To achieve this, it was decided that everything that the Helena Rubinstein Company would develop in the future would be "Fashion White." This concept would symbolize the purity and science that was one half of the "Science of Beauty" and the elegance and fashion sense that was the other.

"Fashion White" is easy to see, but difficult to describe in words. It was shown to the whole Helena Rubinstein organization in a series of pictures, and it was incorporated into advertising, packaging, and even into the lobby of the new offices. In a further step, the following quotation, also from Ruskin, was chosen to define "Fashion White" and was publicized in various ways: "The utmost possible sense of beauty is conveyed by a translucent surface of white and pale warm red, subdued by the most pure and delicate grays, as in the finer portions of the human frame. . . . in wreaths of snow . . . and in white plumage under rose light."

As a result, by 1975 the Helena Rubinstein Company again started to have an over-all corporate "look." It has become the "Fashion White" Company.

4. *Entities*

Madame Rubinstein was reputed never to have introduced a new product without having clearly defined which segment of the population it would appeal to and why. She knew instinctively all her life what marketing executives, with their segmentation studies, psychographics and "reasons why" only discovered in any systematic way after the Second World War; namely, that every product must fill a clearly defined and empty consumer need. When she died, however, new products were no longer introduced for a particular market segment, nor did each product have an exclusive niche. On the contrary, new products were introduced randomly; they cannibalized each other. To avoid this, Helene Rubinstein marketing management established a series of product "entities." An entity was defined as: "(a) a group of consumers, of one psychological type and of a specific age, who have one particular type of cosmetic desire; and (b) a group of products that is technically developed specifically to appeal to that desire."

The lowest-age-group entity is Bio–Clear. It is designed for the seventeen-year-old girl* who has a problem with oily skin, acne, and pimples. It is, therefore, a medicated line consisting of a variety of products designed, to the limits of existing scientific capabilities, to alleviate these typical teen-age skin problems.

Fresh Cover is the next entity. It is for the twenty-five-year-old woman who leads an active life and is just starting to want to use make-up. Its reason for

*One specific age was chosen for the women in each entity. We recognize, of course, that any entity is used by women of more than one age, but we feel that a specific age is easier to envisage for copywriters, product managers, and management. When we define Fresh Cover as being suitable for the twenty-five-year-old woman, that is a clear statement; if we said that it is for women between eighteen and thirty, this would be true, but would make it impossible to pinpoint precisely our advertising. There is, after all, a very great difference between a girl of eighteen and a woman of thirty!

existence: the product is designed to "let your skin breathe." The make-up in the Fresh Cover line is made of a branched-chain molecule which may be described as "porous"; it does indeed allow a greater degree of respiration and perspiration than would be possible with an occlusive, oil-based make-up.

Skin Dew is the entity for the thirty-year-old woman who wishes to protect her skin from further aging. Its formulation contains a milk protein called "Ferments Lactique," which does in fact slow down the aging process.

Helena Rubinstein has eleven entities in all, each specifically formulated for a particular desire within a defined group of women. As a result of the entity principle, all new products developed can now be checked for appropriateness in context with all other products in the line. In other words, the company is now doing what Madame Rubinstein did in her lifetime: judiciously expanding its product line (and its sales)—without treading on its own toes!

5. *One World*

Madame Rubinstein traveled extensively. Wherever she went, she demanded that her products be available, unvarying in appearance, unvarying in quality.

With the world shrinking as a result of the ease of travel and with fashions remarkably uniform throughout the world, Rubinstein product uniformity is even more important. The company has, therefore, reinstituted the "one-world look" of Helena Rubinstein. Every one of its twenty manufacturing subsidiaries operates with the understanding that product quality must rigidly adhere to worldwide specifications. Packaging must be identical; product names must be the same; and the "Fashion White" appearance must be uniform. Even advertising must be identical in concept, although local mores may require changes in the appearance and tone of the advertising.

6. *Savings, Efficiency, and Planning*

Madame Rubinstein was, of course, the very model of the frugal entrepreneur; no waste was possible under her eagle eye and iron control. Today, this personal control has been replaced by careful business planning: five-year plans; savings task forces; cost-of-sales reviews; sophisticated management information systems; inventory- and cash-management controls; and the many other techniques and tools of modern business management that are all part of systematizing Madame Rubinstein's business frugality.

7. *Getting Things Moving*

Madame Rubinstein's greatest contribution was her dynamic leadership. Her very presence stood for progress, innovation, and forward movement. Today, the new Helena Rubinstein Company is regaining that dynamism. Every day there is some new product, some new sales-building plan, some new momentum to be felt. Every executive in the company is contributing to this new inspiration and momentum. What precise chemistry creates it is the subject for another book, but that it exists is obviously so.

Perhaps it is Madame Rubinstein's final gift that, having resuscitated her mystique, today's Helena Rubinstein Company has inherited, too, some of the dynamism that shaped and characterized her whole life.

There is evidence that Helena Rubinstein is undergoing a turnaround that is more than temporary. I believe that it has been possible only because we have learned how to distill into a modern management system the genius, the flamboyance, the mystique of the founder. I believe it is a lesson any company seeking to transmute itself from the private fiefdom of a brilliant entrepreneur into a well-run, professionally managed public company would do well to heed.

Peter Drucker has been frequently quoted to the effect that there is an "absence of any tenable economic theory of business enterprise." Of course he is right. There is no over-all "theory of business." There is just some determined businessman who directs thousands of people to work toward one goal. He generally sets a goal that is sound in business terms, but he chooses it from the many sound alternatives that exist on the basis of his hunch, his preference. He is certainly not going to lose sight of his goal because some overachieving young pup way down in his carefully directed and ritualized organization wishes to shoot for some other goal. Indeed, if organizations were wholly true to their own ideals, there would be only one goal per organization and no overachiever in lower ranks would ever have a chance for achievement of his own. He would either be thrown out very promptly indeed, or he would remain, despite even the most extraordinary struggle, merely a cog running in exact unison with all the other cogs.

Fortunately for the overachiever, however (and fortunately for business too), most businesses are not single-minded in pursuing their stated goal. Businesses are either so large that they can afford to have several and sometimes even flexible goals, or they are small but lack the discipline to adhere exclusively to one goal. Thus, whether or not the establishment of new goals or sub-goals is permissible, it is certainly inevitable. No organization is likely to be able to muster the discipline to remain single-minded for long. It is this inevitability that allows even those overachievers who have not yet reached senior status to find unlimited opportunities.

Philip Morris was pursuing the dual goal of selling more and more cigarettes and making major, unrelated acquisitions to be run as separate entities. The company did not want to build new businesses from scratch. (A wise decision, by the way, since few major corporations are effective at building enterprises from nothing. They drown out the budding enterprise with corporate overheads, and usually place it in the charge of a junior who lacks the needed experience.) In line with these goals, it was Philip Morris's intention to build its small gum and confectionery division by acquisition. Since all there was in the division was Clark Gum, which was too small to exist alone, acquisition was not only the corporate goal, but also obviously the right direction.

Unfortunately, no sooner was the acquisition hunt started, than it became clear that there were no suitable acquisitions available. At that point, had the corporate goals been followed as they should have been, Philip Morris would have either found a way to spin-off the Clark Gum Company, or at least let it lie dormant and unloved where it could do neither harm nor good. Instead, and quite in contradiction to the established corporate goals, it was resolved to build from nothing a new confectionery business and merge it with the Clark Gum Company. Thus, instead of adhering to the corporate goals, unwritten but clearly *felt* by Philip Morris executives, the gum and confectionery division in short order established its own clearly written goals and started to implement them. They developed some fascinating new products (including at least one which was patented); negotiated joint venture agreements with Rowntree of England and Suchard of Switzerland; established successful test markets of three Rowntree Candy Bars, Kit Kat, Aero, and Coffee Crisp; created a gum and confectionery marketing and sales organization; and began developing plans for a new $15 million factory.

Inevitably, however, progress was laborious because this sort of growth from within was contrary to the over-all corporate goals: internal growth for cigarettes; growth by acquisition for everything else. Because the gum and confectionery division failed to adhere to these goals, it was a deviation, a pleasure/pain irritation in the side of the corporate giant that sometimes pleased it but at other times proved a trial and a nuisance.

The question of whether the corporation was benefited or harmed by being pushed forward into a new venture by that little group of candy men who made up the gum and confectionery division is a fascinating one—partly because it cannot be answered. On the one hand, since a great deal of management time and effort was forced into the candy venture, it is quite possible that it represented an undesirable expenditure of corporate energy. On the other hand, had the company continued its efforts, I believe it would today enjoy a major and very profitable confectionery business. By this time, I believe, instead of having sold its Rowntree franchise to Hershey, it would have converted its candy business into a further major thrust for the company; and that thrust in turn would no doubt have become institutionalized, "goalized"—and become part of the corporate religion—so that no new group of young men could, without tremendous effort, take over the candy division and turn it in a new direction, for example, toward the manufacture of cookies. Cookies, you see, had been decreed early in the division's history as different, and incompatible with the marketing of candy!

There is no doubt that creating action without being disruptive is and will remain one of the greatest problems—and challenges—to the overachievers in industry. But it may be that, as large companies become huge and huge companies become what my children call gi-normous—and as they consequently become more and more decentralized—there will be more "swinging room" for the young overachiever. It remains true that, to move forward without chaos, an organization must maintain considerable uniformity of direction. However, it is also true —and wonderfully heartening—that any man who is sufficiently determined and, importantly, cheerful, can create new and constructive forward motion if he really wants to. Finding some imaginative solutions often helps too!

A young businessman who worked for a company making cosmetics and hair-care products decided that his firm should get into the cosmetic-appliance field and should manufacture such small appliances as electric hair curlers, face massagers, and water piks.

"That's not our business." "We don't know anything about the appliance business." "We haven't got a suitable service organization." "Our sales force doesn't call on small-appliance dealers." These and a myriad of other apparently sound objections were brought up by his management. "But," added one of the more aggressive of the directors, "maybe you can find a compromise to move us rather gradually in that direction."

The young businessman listened carefully—and then developed a careful and clever plan. First, and with the enthusiastic support of his management, he started selling a mix-it-yourself hair-dye kit for hairdressers who wanted to develop a special color formula for each customer in order to keep the customer loyal to their salons. Soon sales of this mix-it-yourself arrangement were substantial. But the hairdressers had a complaint. They found mixing the dyes from many little bottles to be a messy procedure, and they wanted an automatic way to mix; they also wanted a way to retain automatically the information on precisely what mixture had been used for each customer. There is nothing worse, the hairdressers insisted, than to convince a customer that "Viridian Silver with a touch of Auburn Bronze" is the "only" color for her—and then to forget prior to her next visit what you told her, and how you make Viridian Silver! The young man was not in the least surprised and quickly unveiled a new machine which the company's R and D department had meantime developed. It replaced the messy little bottles and mixed the colors rather like the Sunoco variant-octane gas pumps, and it recorded them. It was a small electrical machine and it worked very nicely. Naturally, it was enthusiastically received both by the hairdressing trade, and, equally importantly, by corporate management who had now been given a way to enter the small-appliance business without most of the negatives they had envisioned for the business in the first place. The appliance, after all, was now well within the main thrust of their hair-products business. But, at the same time, a new goal had been set. Thereafter expansion into other appliances was a relatively easy matter.

A young friend of mine felt that his company, which was in the candy business, should move into making and marketing ice cream. It was a small, conservatively run company and change was anathema.

"No," his management emphasized. "You know nothing about freezing technology or about marketing ice cream. Moreover, you are Vice President of Operations and you shouldn't be worrying about what new businesses we should be entering. Get back to your factories!"

My friend smiled cheerfully and started an industrial-ingredients business selling candy chips to ice cream manufacturers. This was within the area of his responsibility and had the approval of his boss. Within a year, the business was so successful that he was able to set up a full research and development laboratory specializing in ice cream additives. He and his people soon knew everything there was to know about freezing technology. Again, he suggested moving into the retail ice cream business.

"No," his management repeated. "If we did that we might antagonize our new customers for ice cream ingredients and lose the nice profitable business you built for us."

My friend smiled his smile . . . and instead obtained approval to enter into a joint-venture agreement with a company not in the ice cream business whereby he supplied the ingredients and made the ice cream, and they supplied the marketing and selling effort. The new joint-venture company was owned equally by the two partners. Within a year, it was a major factor in the retail ice cream industry.

"Now," said my friend triumphantly to his management, "will you believe that we should be in the business of marketing ice cream?"

"Oh no!" said his management. "For then we might antagonize our partner in the joint venture." They paused. "But we would like to find a way to increase profits and if you could find a way. . . ." they trailed off weakly.

My friend's smile must have been a little forced by that time. But he is an overachiever par excellence and he made his final bid.

"I'm sorry," he said to his partner, "but I have to raise my ice cream-making prices. We need more profits."

"If you do that," the partner responded, "we'll be forced out of business."

"Then we'll simply have to acquire your share of the partnership instead," my friend said. And that is what happened!

Only three years after his company had told him unequivocally that, for good enough reason, they would not enter the ice cream business under any circumstances—and that he should stick to running his factories—my friend had built his company into one of the major manufacturers and marketers in the ice cream industry.

Tenacity and good cheer are vital. Swimming against the stream of corporate tradition can result in many terribly hurt feelings among the downstream swimmers. But those hurts should never be exacerbated by personal nastiness, coldness, or insensitivity. Organizations must be sold new ideas, not bullied into them. Most overachievers are dedicated, stubborn, and opinionated. But most, too, are delightful fellows.

As big business continues to grow, new techniques, new ideas, new types of motivation are needed. One of the most important is the growing need to create consensus. Rarely is a man very successful if he cannot move men to think together and act alike. Some do it with golden-tongued glibness, others through personal warmth and disarming candor, and still others by laying down, sometimes even in writing, a path that seems to have such irrefutable logic that none can deviate from it. The teachings are many, but the results are always the same: the group involved moves forward in unison. It *wants* to move forward together But the desire for the consent of all, for achievement through consensus, may not be as new as at first sight it might seem. Even tyrants have always required that their men be loyal—rather than be forced to be loyal. Still, management for achievement is not and will not be a group function. One man, the overachiever, will set the policies. He will create the desire for consensus among all those who are needed for implementation.

I believe it is one of the most dramatically wrong business views, but unfortunately one that is perpetuated in writing and speeches throughout the business community, that business management is a team function. "*A* manager can only perform as well as the *people* who report to him," writes Emery in a rather pompous and in my view thoroughly wrongheaded book called *The Compleat Manager.* It is a point he emphasizes throughout the book. But if it were true, it would be the most certain guarantee that nothing would ever get done! Like the logical extension of any fatalistic philosophy, it would entirely destroy incentive. Were Emery's view right, and were it extended to its logical although perhaps exaggerated conclusion, the chief executive officer of a major corporation could perform nothing more than could his vice presidents, who in turn could do no more than their managers, who in turn could do no more than their employees. Ultimately, the entire organization would spend all its time training each other, and achievement would be limited to the ability of the most lowly janitor! Emery tries to offset this obvious fallacy by pointing out the importance of goal setting.

Here he is right. Undoubtedly, setting goals is one of the most important tasks facing any achievement-oriented businessman. But then Emery eliminates even that fail-safe by supporting yet another widely held fallacy: that priorities should be established to differentiate the "desired" from the "required" goals. He describes "required" goals as being the obvious essentials: staying in business, staying solvent, staying alive. The result is that all other goals—getting something new started, getting a new product introduced, building—are merely "desired" goals, not essential ones. Action becomes a second priority, and innovation a luxury which is nice to have but not essential. The result, zero achievement!

It is astounding to me how widely the fallacy of "action through teamwork" is quoted. It has become a truly dangerous business platitude—but fortunately only that, not a truth. In the real business world it is a leader who sets the pace and the team that follows. "The distance between the leaders and averages are constant," writes Peter Drucker. I doubt whether this is wholly true either, but it is at least useful.

The fact is, that below the level of genius, achievement depends more on the courage to trust in success than on the ability to do research. As Harlan Cleveland points out, "The executive must always be ready to supply a pinch of unwarranted optimism to the stew of calculated costs."

Akin to the priorities fallacy so neatly, if inadvertently, summarized by Emery, is the information fallacy which, again, is perpetuated by the plethora of textbooks on decision making. Simply stated, the preachers of this view say that, in order to make a correct decision, it is necessary to know all the facts. Like many widely perpetuated fallacies, this one has considerable surface plausibility. "How can you make a decision if you don't know what you're talking about?" is obviously a good question. The point is, however, that whenever the decision involves new directions, new thoughts, new initiatives, *you cannot possibly know all the facts.* That is why "experts" can be so debilitating to achievement. "Gloom and reluctance are the trademarks of expertise," writes Harlan Cleveland, talking directly to my heart. The fact is that many men prefer the protection of their expertise to the risks inherent in leadership. "It is far easier," Cleveland explains, "to be an expert, with the obligation merely to be right, than to be a leader, with the obligation to fuse a dozen forms of rigid rectitude into relevant action."

The point is that whenever men set a new course, or explore in a new direction, they are entering undiscovered territories; the facts are, by definition, unknown at the start. There is more delay, I suggest, from trying to gather unknowable facts before making a decision than from any other cause. The right way to make a decision, the activist's way, is to decide what you want to do . . . and then, gathering all the *available* facts, determine first whether what you want is possible or, second, if it is not possible on the basis of the facts you have, how to modify them or create new ones that make your choice possible.

There is a wonderful essay written by Edgar Allen Poe purporting to describe how he came to write his famous poem, "The Raven." With apparent seriousness, he describes how he wished to write a melancholy poem and therefore needed a melancholy sound. He chose the sound "or." Next he needed a word which was the ultimate in melancholia and which incorporated the vowel sound he had chosen. What better word than "nevermore"? Then he needed a symbol of melancholy which could legitimately make the vowel sound "or" and use the word "nevermore." The only possible symbol which fulfilled these requirements was, of course, a black raven. So, step by step—and with a wonderfully straight face—Poe asks us to believe that he created "The Raven"—its meter and rhythm, its content, and its heroine, Lenore (which name is melancholy, incorporates the vowel "or" and is pronounceable by a raven), by a logical analysis of the facts.

Anyone who has ever mustered the determination to get something done and has modified or created the facts to make it possible must laugh up his sleeve, convinced that Poe must have written "The Raven" first and rationalized it later.

Decision making is easy for the overachiever. He usually knows intuitively what he wants to do. He quickly gathers what facts there are and makes up his mind on the basis of those facts —or, if he remains convinced that his intuition was right, in the teeth of them. Then, if necessary, he creates the additional facts he needs to fulfill the objective he intuitively and perhaps impetuously set. Machiavelli, who can hardly be remembered as a man who moved without checking the facts, the political realities—and practically everything else—nevertheless wrote: "On the whole, I judge impetuosity to be better than caution."

Decision making is a vital ingredient in the overachiever's ability to create action. But for him it is relatively easy to make a decision because he has three fundamental characteristics which make it so:

First, he has the hungry man's scorn for the very idea that it "can't be done."

Second, he has a fair measure of what Harlan Cleveland calls "unwarranted optimism." (Unwarranted in this context does not mean unjustified. It simply means an optimism for which the facts are not *yet* available.)

Third, he has the "impetuosity" (or, in my terms, the courage) Machiavelli admires.

Most of the writing on decision making misses the basic point that to make the right decision often and fast enough takes more guts than facts. That is the challenge to the overachiever. That is the difficulty he faces. But it is also the opportunity he enjoys.

It is the willingness of the overachiever to make gut decisions that sets him free. Writes Cleveland: "The function of the executive is to make the difficult choices others are reluctant to make. And in any society those who choose the most have the most reason to feel free."

The name Machiavelli brings to mind one of the most difficult problems facing any man and particularly any overachieving man. It is the fundamental philosophical question of whether the means needed for achievement are justified by the ends of the achievement itself. The question hits at the heart of one of the fundamental problems of humanity. Whether we consider Goethe's Faust enrolling the devil as his personal servant, or Nietzsche's violent amorality, we always comes back to the fundamental question of whether good can emerge from evil.

One of the most frightening ironies of modern history and, therefore, of our daily lives, is that our inheritance from Adolf Hitler and his Nazis, perhaps the most evil group the world has ever known, includes several of the greatest benefits the world possesses. Penicillin, space rocketry, atomic energy, and the State of Israel are merely some of the apparent results of World War II. The thought is of course the more frightening when one recognizes that Christ, a symbol of man's understanding of good, could be given the blame for a vast amount of misery and destruction perpetrated during a thousand religious fights. "If one is going to live one's life literally and totally by the sermon on the Mount or Dhammapada, and one cannot manage to be a saint, one will end by making a sorry mess of oneself," writes William Barrett in what may be the definitive study of modern existential philosophy, *The Irrational Man.*

This is a problem of philosophy so weighty that I do not find the time nor do I see in myself the wisdom to try to resolve it here. Fortunately, however, the question can be circumvented for the business overachiever. The fact is that in the environment of business, I can think of no instance in my experience in which means not commensurate with our normal standards of morality were justified from a practical point of view. In the business community immorality, dishonesty, double dealing rarely, if ever, result in the desired ends in the long term. A lie may have the short-term advantage of achieving the desired action, but business achievement rests so much on personal reputations that I doubt whether the liar will be able to move forward very far. There has been a great deal written about the universality of dishonesty among businessmen who have achieved gigantic success. Aristotle Onassis stood accused of having founded his fortune on illegally marketing cigarettes under a competitor's name; perhaps the story is true, perhaps not. But it was not the essence of Onassis's success. He would have become just as successful if he had never heard of tobacco, because he was the epitome of an overachiever. I agree that in many overachievers there is a degree of ruthlessness, but it is directed toward others of their own size. It is a "guts" ruthlessness: the manifestation of enormous courage and enormous hunger. I have found that men of great achievement are not dishonest or unkind or unfeeling to the weak. I can find no evidence that there is a correlation between dishonesty and achievement; in fact, I find the opposite. Even Machiavelli (the very name symbolizes amorality) emphasized that "we cannot attribute to fortune or virtue that which [is] . . . achieved without either." Coming from a bitter man whose reward for striving to improve his country's position was exile and who consistently purported to believe that goodness has no place in the lives of princes, this is a remarkably strong, although probably unconscious, endorsement of the value of goodness in context with power and renown.

We have reached the point at which it is time to summarize how action is forced in business. There are, I believe, six parts to the creation of action in a business organization:

The first is to create, not on the basis of all the facts, but on the basis of the *available* facts—plus hunch and a good deal of courage—a new goal.

The second is to create around that goal-in-fact a sense of purpose and agreement among all the organization's people.

The third is part of the second: to clothe that goal in quasi-religious terms so that, to the organization as a whole, it becomes *more* than just a goal or a consensus belief. Rather it is elevated to become a purpose, almost an individual need.

The fourth, surprisingly, is to be a charming fellow of good cheer and down-to-earth niceness. This remains one of the most effective ways of achieving consensus.

The fifth is to make things fun to do, to create enjoyment among the people of the organization. Without enjoyment nothing will ultimately get done.

But the sixth remains the ultimate necessity for action. It is simply that you must maintain an unalterable determination to get things done and a deeply held conviction and understanding of the fact that most harm is done by not doing. "Throughout history it has been the inaction of those who could have acted, the indifference of those who should have known better, the silence of the voice of justice when it mattered most, that has made it possible for evil to triumph," are words of considerable wisdom written by Haile Selassie. In precisely the same way it has usually been such a lack of action which has been the cause when "do-nothingness" has triumphed over innovation in the business world.

One successful man described his view of how to get things done:

"First try opening the door by turning the handle," he said. "If that doesn't work, try a key. Failing that, break the door down. If you can't, get in by a window."

"What happens if everything fails?" a young listener interrupted.

The great overachiever responded instantly and with total sincerity, "That is totally unthinkable," he said.

The Overachiever
as a Scaler of Pyramids

A well-run business organization must fight the tendency to develop a life of its own that then dominates the thought and action of its members.

The growing subsidiary of a large American company in Canada used to sell its employees tickets to its cafeteria. By tradition, sale of the tickets was on Mondays only, and the chore was assigned to a different secretary every week. The tickets were standard rolls of theater tickets, oblong, with corners rounded inward to facilitate tearing, and read "Admit One." They had originally been chosen because they were cheap and readily available. As the company expanded, the women could no longer handle the Monday crowd. To solve this problem, it was decided to select an automatic ticket-dispensing machine. A variety of them was marketed.

"Please find a machine which will dispense our lunch tickets," said the office manager to one of his more completely indoctrinated junior executives.

The young man searched diligently for a dispenser; but he soon found that there was none on the market capable of handling oblong tickets with inward-rounded corners. Instead, working determinedly but unthinkingly toward his absurd objective—presumably with the agreement of a substantial body of people in the corporation—the young executive spent $10,000 on developing a new machine capable of dispensing this particular type of ticket.

Jack Grimm, Vice President and General Manager of Colgate–Palmolive's European Division, tells a particularly pithy story of corporate life. It appears that, in order to avoid theft of their small, electronic desk calculators, Colgate's security department installed into its machines a buzzer-alarm that rings loudly as soon as the machine is lifted off the desk. Also, since Colgate is a sensibly frugal company, they limit the number of such calculators to the minimum needed and tell their financial trainees to share them.

Imagine then, the view from Jack's corner office as a young trainee sprints across the general office, dodging athletically between desks and scattering papers and secretaries in his wake, clutching under his arm a loudly buzzing calculator!

This sort of entrenched thinking, or nonthinking, is an ever-present danger in any vast human organization. Joseph Heller's classic book of army life, *Catch 22,* deals with little else. Up to a point it is a necessary form of regimentation. Without such thinking-in-unison, no organization could act in unison; instead, every individual would shoot off in a different direction and then ricochet from task to task and goal to goal. The whole organization would fall into kinetic confusion. And, of course, this is a situation in which the overachiever can play a crucial role, for he is the man who recognizes the standard trend of thought as being useful, but neither everlasting nor inevitable. He is the successful deviant thinker who clearly appreciates the need for change and who can implement it with as little disruption as possible.

Nevertheless, it is certain that nothing new can get done if *some* men do not deviate in their thoughts. By definition, any organization which thinks in unison and acts in unison can do so only along a noninnovative path.

Successful deviant thinking is one route to the top, but it is by no means the only route. There are several other ways to attain success within any organizational structure. Each involves a degree of achievement, of course, but not necessarily overachievement. Nevertheless, in order to differentiate between overachievement and these other modes of rising to or near the top in business, they are worth investigating.

The most frequent path to the top—perhaps not to the ultimate pinnacle but rather to a high plateau—is *know thy procedure book*! It is the first commandment of corporate life—and a very valuable one. There are many men who have risen to the position of vice president in a major company simply by knowing this bible of the "unison thinking" of the corporation more completely than their peers—and adhering to it more fervently. It is often a laudable approach. For one thing, when times are good and no change is needed or even desirable, it virtually prevents the executive from making major mistakes. Innovation, while sometimes essential and often desirable, is always dangerous. Adhering to the procedure book is safe as long as the book remains appropriate. Of course, if the corporate procedure book becomes out of date and therefore wrong, then following it is no excuse for failure. More usually, however, the corporation moves with success along the procedural path predetermined, of course, by some earlier overachiever. Deservedly, with it moves its servant, occasionally to a very high peak indeed.

Unfortunately for him, this man is sometimes moved so high that he reaches a position where existing procedures are inappropriate. For example, he may be promoted to a job which did not previously exist. Then he fails quickly and certainly.

A successful young businessman was promoted to vice president of his corporation's Brazilian subsidiary. His task was to launch the company on a certain business venture of a type well established in New York but new in Brazil. After only a few months the head of the subsidiary concluded he was hopeless; not just poor or inexperienced, quite hopeless! He simply had no idea what to do next. His decisions were rare and wrong. His leadership abysmal. Even his appearance was sloppy. Finally, in total frustration at not seeing the new venture starting, the Brazilian manager recommended to his head office in New York that the man be dismissed.

"We're most surprised to hear you say that our man is ineffectual," New York management responded. "When he was back here in New York, he was always so good doing things just the way we wanted them. He was so experienced in our methods that we were sure that he could be effective in implementing our way of doing this sort of business in Brazil."

The problem was immediately obvious. In his new position, the man had to build a business from scratch. There was no existing organization. To his consternation, he found that he simply did not know what to do next.

This is, of course, one example of Dr. Lawrence Peter's "Peter Principle." The Brazilian vice president suffered from the same syndrome of "procedure-captivity" as did Dr. Peter's "Miss Ditto," who continued to teach her class as the room slowly filled with water because she didn't hear the emergency-bell signal.

Following the procedure book perfectly is neither unnecessary nor easy and often it is well rewarded. But far greater is the achiever who can establish a new corporate procedure book for future underlings to follow. Alfred Sloan, who I described as the genius who established the organizational structure of General Motors, was such a man. As he explained with pride, his greatest achievement was the establishment of effective procedures. In a similar view, Robert Heller writes, "Men like Simon Marks [the genius behind the huge and profitable English retail firm, Marks & Spencer], for all their pervasive personalities, are so deeply interested in organization that . . . they express their egos through the systems they built." Lord Marks, Alfred Sloan—one could cite McNamara of Ford as easily—are of that breed of men that does not follow procedures but creates them.

A third path upward in the giant corporation is that used by the "contact man." He knows everyone; he is loved by everyone; he has myriad friends and no enemies; and he can obtain favors on the basis of "who he knows." Usually, of course, he is the scion of a well-known family. Or, as Ogden Nash put it in "The Terrible People": "Some people's money is merited, and other people's is inherited." But not always.

One well-known chief financial officer who can be seen most days eating lunch at "21"—and with great frequency, dinner as well—(and where, typically, he is loved by the owners) is a poor boy who made good. He holds his position as senior vice president of finance in a billion-dollar plus company as a reward. He joined the company many years ago when it was in deep financial trouble. There was no cash. There was less credit. All there was was incipient desperation. It was his banking friends—and his prematurely white hair, courtly Southern manner and total honesty—that allowed the company to obtain the one further loan it needed for survival. Thereafter, with money in the till, an aggressive new management, and at least one superbly successful new product, the company turned around and has been growing fast and profitably ever since. It would not have survived without him, but with him, survive it did—and he has been in highly paid employed retirement ever since. In a sense, of course, his was a very major achievement indeed.

The best contact of all—at least for many men of less than outstanding capacities—is to marry the boss's daughter. Whether marriage is an easy path, however, lies in the eye of the beholder. Certainly, some of the ladies who were wooed and won more for the charms of their fathers' fortunes than for their own are such shrews that their husbands' marital contributions must be considered as an overachievement of remarkable magnitude! In Germany, a country that habitually takes things to their extremes—and frequently tips the baby out with the bath water—marrying the boss's daughter is a highly organized activity. Many German newspapers, from tabloids to the most stolid and dignified, carry columns of want ads in which ladies of little beauty, impeccable although not necessarily voluntary virtue, and certain rich compensating assets are offered to bright prospective husbands as part of a more or less blatantly stated business deal. The advertisements are, incidentally, sad to a degree, and so glowingly written that our Federal Communications Commission would see in them little "truth in advertising."

Another not infrequent route to the top (for those who choose to marry purely for love) is to find a new product created by someone else—and ride it to the sky.

One bright young product manager in the Canadian subsidiary of a large American consumer-goods company took his first step upward by begging to be made product manager in charge of a brand about to be introduced into the Canadian market—a brand that had already been fabulously successful in the United States. Its almost inevitable success in Canada, where it was a carbon copy of the American product and marketing plan, assured him of rapid promotion.

Of course, recognizing the right product is a tremendous achievement in its own right.

An acquaintance of mine claims steadfastly that he was once offered a job by a small company that had decided to challenge Gillette in the razor blade business. They claimed they had a better blade and would soon have a huge business. Unfortunately, they explained, they could not pay very much at the start; instead they would give him a share of the profits that were generated under his marketing leadership—quite a sizable share.

"I was intrigued for a moment," he told me. "But when the name of the company was mentioned, I laughed and lost all further interest. Of all the unlikely things! The company was a tiny little English outfit that made swords —Wilkinson swords!"

As Francis Bacon puts it in his essay "Of Innovations," "As the births of leading creatures at first are ill-shapen, so are all innovations." But, adds Bacon, "he that will not apply new remedies must expect new evils." Perhaps my friend should have read Bacon more assiduously!

The ability to create consensus is, as I have mentioned, another effective route forward. The modern business organization is so huge that there may be different factions, possibly with incompatible objectives. Each of them is probably the fiefdom of some charming but determined overachiever and, since they cannot compromise or cooperate, each seeks to establish its course as the dominant one. As a result, the organization may be in danger of smashing itself to pieces. Even if the leaders of each faction recognize the danger, they may be unable to do anything about it. If this is the case, then a man who, with wisdom and calm, can step into their breach and, time and again, restore peace and suggest a road practical to all is invaluable. It is a rare man who can parlay such a peacemaking ability into long-term success. For one thing, a company made up of factions with fundamentally differing objectives, however carefully they compromise, remains an organization in unstable equilibrium. Sooner or later one faction will become dominant and the others will cease to exist. At that point, there is no longer any need for a peacemaker. His role, even if successful, is generally a very short-lived one. Nevertheless, this quality of peacemaking, particularly if it is combined with other strengths, has proven useful in a number of cases.

Loyalty and longevity (plus being a nice guy, often coupled with the role of mediator discussed above) is a path that just a few men are able to follow to positions of influence. Usually these assets are combined either with family connections or with the knack of holding yourself loyal not to certain people but (if the word loyalty applies) to an upward trend.

The national sales manager of one candy company, Stan, was a man of this type. Slowly but surely he worked his way up the ladder of at least limited success by being nice to everyone. If you needed an errand run, Stan would take care of it. If you were having trouble finding a golf game out of town on a week end, you could call Stan and he could arrange it by long-distance telephone with the pro at the local club. At Christmas Stan would never forget to send you an attractive silk tie. If you wanted to track down a rumor—or to create a new one—Stan was your man. As a result, he always sold a little bit of extra candy because he was loved. And, day in and day out, that is what he worked at: being loved!

On the other hand, hitching your wagon to one particular star, a man who seems destined inevitably to reach the top, is another viable technique for success. "Making the strength of the boss productive is a key to the subordinate's own effectiveness," writes Peter Drucker. I don't suggest that you do not need ability as well. Every one of these techniques for scaling the business pyramid requires a substantial level of achievement. Even if overachievement is not always necessary, some ability is always essential.

Which brings us back once again to the surest way of all to achieve real success: to engineer it by making something happen, by being an overachiever.

If Overachievers Fail

Even though the most successful overachievers are tactful men who do not disrupt healthy organizations unnecessarily, others are so driven to achievement that they may not be easy to cradle within a large organization. Such men, particularly before they learn the value of motivating a large organization without disrupting it, are full of jagged edges, constantly determined to awaken their peers (and their bosses), and doggedly insistent on getting things done at any price. As a result they are often rejected and not infrequently fired.

When Paul Ange, a French–Canadian graduate of McGill University in Montreal, first went looking for a job a few weeks before graduation, he was interviewed by a large and, as it turned out, rather tired Canadian consumer-goods company. The interview was a group affair in which several job candidates were seen concurrently by several directors of the corporation. Each candidate in turn was asked some broad questions about Canadian culture and each gave polite, superficial answers. Paul, however, sat there becoming more impatient by the second.

Finally it was his turn. Addressing the senior director present, he said: "Frankly, if I answered that question now I would be able to provide you only with more of the same sort of platitudes that you have already heard. I would, however, be very pleased to prepare a detailed paper on the subject and present it to you next week."

There was a stunned silence. One of the outside directors on the company's board sat up and said suddenly, "What's your name?" The others, however, remained silent and looked either stubborn or shocked.

Later, my friend was taken aside by the corporation's employment director. "You seem somewhat too aggressive for our company," said the director.

But the next post brought a job offer from the outside director. "Now that you have been turned down by this company, I feel free to offer you a job in my organization," the letter read in part. "You are precisely the type of aggressive and action-oriented man our company needs and wants."

An aggressive product manager working for a major consumer-goods company managed to build the share of his brand against the vigorous opposition of competitive products by running an exceptional number of promotions, including several novel consumer contests backed by new forms of in-store display. To do all this—and still move with enough speed to outflank the competition—he broke many corporate rules: sales material did not reach the salesmen on time; form 33/K-24B, which ought to have been filled out six weeks in advance of start of promotion, was never filled out at all; recommendations that should have been approved by twenty-three people were implemented prior to any approval; and, worse, there were considerable cost overruns. He was, of course, fully aware of these violations, but he considered them so minor that he remained unconcerned—even when he was told that he would be called before a committee of inquiry. His advance information had told him that his brand's share had finally risen. For five years the share had declined; now, for the first time in the memory of all but the most senior members of the company, the share of this particular brand had started to move upward. He was sure that the committee of inquiry would share his delight and that he would walk away praised as a hero, not castigated as a miscreant.

Imagine his amazement when, after using his brand's turnaround to justify his misdemeanors, he was told icily by the senior manager present: "That is completely beside the point."

In my view his superior was probably right. While the product manager's achievement in building the brand was real, the disruption he caused was probably great; moreover, it was unnecessary. He could surely have built the brand in the same way three weeks later and filled in every form, attained every clearance, and shipped every sales aid.

No business can afford a man, however constant his achievement, if that achievement carries with it constant, excessive disruption. The overachiever who does not learn when to rock the boat and when not to may well deserve the notice of termination he will undoubtedly receive. On the other hand, it is lamentably true that even the most mature and careful activist may, on some occasions, without cause or justification beyond his penchant for disturbing the *status quo,* find himself in difficulties and either be forced to resign or actually be fired.

Halbert E. Payne never had a failure. He resuscitated Procter and Gamble of Canada, Ltd., when it was staffed by spritely yearlings untrained—and quite unsuccessful—at their task. He dramatically improved the Jello Division of General Foods. He spent a year at Clairol and developed for that company a series of excellent new products. And yet he was eventually forced out of each one of these companies. For he shook the tree, he created action, he was a dynamo all of the time. Ultimately, he became too much for the companies who initially benefited so greatly by his presence. They rejected him, just as the body of the patient, be it ever so in need of a new heart, nevertheless rejects the transplant.

Overachievers, like all other employees, fight against this sort of elimination—except that they usually fight more effectively. The best overachievers are most careful to work their changes and improvements within the organization, disrupting it as little as possible. It is not that the overachiever is afraid of being fired or of the world of the unemployed. It is simply that achievement *in absentia* is a contradiction in terms. The overachiever, therefore, usually learns to give in on minor matters in order to achieve his major ends. "Never be a martyr over your clothing," my father used to tell me. "Dress inconspicuously and you can change the world without anyone noticing!"

Compromise fails and action ends when the writing is on the wall—or on the pink slip! It is at that moment that the overachiever is forced to move on. The question is, what happens then?

The happy answer is that he usually remains highly successful.

Halbert Payne is head of his own marketing consulting firm, in tremendous demand and earning huge fees. Whether you are in Mexico City, Tokyo, or Hamburg, Hal Payne, full of ebullient charm, surrounded by controversy and action—and enjoying every minute of it—is likely to be there.

One of the classic examples of the rejection and subsequent reacceptance of an exceptional overachiever is that of Theodore Vail, who became President of the Bell Telephone System some time before 1900 and started advocating two incredible innovations. First he said that the business of Bell was service as distinct from pure profit making. Businessmen today recognize their responsibilities as public servants; the utilities in particular have long emphasized the public-service aspects of their businesses. But when Vail suggested that Bell Telephone should provide service even if it was not to the immediate profit of the corporation, he was treated with incredulity and ostracized as a pariah and worse. When he also suggested that some form of government regulation was inevitable and even desirable, provided that it was not too stringent, he shocked his audience almost beyond recovery. At a time when regulation was thought to be a dastardly socialist plot, this view, espoused by the President of Bell Telephone Company, was totally outrageous. For promulgating such beliefs, he was fired by Bell's Board of Directors. But the demand for nationalizing Bell grew, and in 1909 Theodore Vail was called back to make Bell into the private monopoly it remains today, the only private monopoly existing in America. He was successful only because he was able to base Bell firmly on the two principles of service and restricted regulation that he had preached originally.

Chusid, one of the larger employment agencies in the United States, used to run an advertisement headlined, "How to Be Fired Successfully." The wording of the advertisement implied that being fired was almost an advantage. Surprisingly, it may be—provided that you are fired for over, not underachievement; provided too that your prospective new employer is convinced that you are an overachiever, not a perennial trouble maker. No company is interested in employing a spoiled corporate brat.

Nevertheless, being fired, even in the most worthy of circumstances and for the most self-confident of men, is a traumatic experience. Inevitably the man must ask himself: "Did I perhaps fail through incompetence after all? Did I wreak havoc unnecessarily? Can I be successful elsewhere without compromising my need for action? Am I as good as I thought I was?" Since no man is perfect, some of the answers must be, "Yes, it was partly my fault." There has to be in all mortals at least some crack of self-doubt which, left alone, may widen to a chasm of neurosis. The overachiever turns from trauma to action and, where the standard businessman may go to pieces, the overachiever ignores his doubts and plunges forward. While the standard businessman, searching desperately for a procedure book to guide him, reads literature on how to be reemployed, the overachiever looks for several new jobs from which to choose.

Two vice presidents were fired on the same day from a small company where, working as a team, they had become too dominant for the weakling who was president and who, not coincidentally, was part of the owning family. In the two months thereafter, the man who had been the tough-minded leader of the two had managed to have twenty-three job interviews; publish an article in *Advertising Age* which brought his name to the attention of the employment community as being both available and extraordinarily talented; complete a $5,000 consulting contract; and accept the best of four excellent job offers. The other man had also been a vice president. He had been paid comparably, had enjoyed an equally good reputation, was of about the same age, had followed a comparable career path and had a resumé that was just as attractive. Outwardly, he seemed just as capable of finding a job. But during the same period of time he had been interviewed only four times, had no job, had taken to staying home most days and painting his house, and had gained about twenty pounds. He did eventually find a pretty good position, but it took him years to regain his full self-confidence.

So difficult and depressing to most men is losing their jobs that many companies, forced by circumstances to fire good and loyal employees, retain consultants who specialize in helping terminated employees adjust to their new circumstances and summon up the determination to find a new job. No overachiever needs such help.

Any man who is fired must question himself. It is not the questioning but the quality of the answers that differentiates the overachiever from the pack. The ordinary man will tend to answer that he was inadequate or, if he is of stubborn mold, will determine to improve himself in the future. When he does find a new job, he will tend to avoid dangerous decisions and will act with timid care. The extraordinary man will evaluate the situation more clearly and will seek to determine whether he or the organization was inadequate. Finding, as he usually will, that it was both, he will do two things: first, vow to overcome his own shortcomings; and second, try to associate himself with a company that is readier for him. When he joins it he will continue undeviatingly to seek to improve it. Perhaps his earlier bad experience will teach him how to achieve such change with less generation of heat; but his zeal for change will not have been diminished and his fear of having his ejection repeated will be weaker than his desire for improvement. To see a man become afraid to act is pathetic.

One business executive, a man of dedication and ability, had done extremely well in a $200 million Midwestern food company. As a result, he was hired by a billion-dollar New York maker of beverages at an exorbitant salary. The politics in his new company were Byzantine; the sums of money he was required to control enormous; the whole place was simply too much for him. In nine months he was out of a job.

Summoning up his ultimate resources, he did manage rapidly to find another job. But there his strength ended. From that day forth, his questioning was never, "What is the right course of action?" but always, "What is the safe course? What would my boss want me to do? What will he approve? What will he agree with?" The poor man worried himself to an ulcer. His marriage disintegrated. He lacked not competence but confidence. His performance in his job, which called for fast, decisive action, was so unsatisfactory that, after two years, his boss, a wise and sensitive man, told him that the company had decided to keep him employed for only another six to nine months. The executive was of course desperate at the thought of having to find another job, but at least he now had nothing to lose in his existing one. Suddenly the pressure for keeping his job and its consequent anxiety was off him. Instead of worrying constantly about what his boss would like, he simply did what he thought right. Immediately his operation improved—even though he remained terribly concerned about finding a new job, and job-hunting took up a great deal of his time.

At the end of four months, his boss said that they had decided to retain him after all because he had demonstrated an ability to get the job done. The executive has never looked back.

Many men who choose the path of action, of innovation, of achievement fail or almost fail at some point in their careers. That is not to say that they inevitably get fired or go broke; these extremes elude most good men. It *is* to say, however, that the frustrations of large organizations—or the tremendous limitations of small ones—not infrequently force even the most persuasive and successful doer to admit to himself that there is nothing left for him to do, that he has reached an action impasse. The action-oriented achiever tends to recognize such an impasse for what it is very quickly, and as fast, he moves on. There is no point, he feels, in simply marking time; and less in battering his cranium against a wall.

About eight years ago, a thirty-year-old actionist resigned from a large corporation. He was well thought of and had been marked for gradual progress up the organizational ladder. His resignation was contrary to the plans of his superiors. They tried to persuade him to stay.

"You can't leave now," they insisted. "For one thing, in only about a year you will become vested in your profit-sharing plan. It will be worth almost fifteen thousand dollars, equaling almost nine months' salary. It will be an excellent bonus for you."

The young man had harbored some doubts before this conversation. But after it, he had none.

"Never," he explained, "would I sell nine months of my life for fifteen thousand bucks. I only have one life to live. I cannot waste or sell its time."

"Would you have stayed at any price?" he was asked.

"Yes," he replied. "If there had been enough money to let me make up for the lost time later."

It was a good reply and one with which most overachievers would agree. The life of almost every successful businessman— or perhaps of every successful man in any field—illustrates above all the full usage of time. To waste it, such men would feel, might be the greatest sin of all. Whether one looks at the great corporation chiefs or the great entrepreneurs, one invariably discovers that they demonstrate an incredible love for work, for work leads to action; and action, above all else, is their ambition.

It is a characteristic of the man of achievement that once he decides that he cannot make progress with reasonable speed however hard he works, he quits at once. Not for him is the agonizing decision of whether leaving is the right thing or the wrong; he simply knows that when the action stops, he must leave. It follows that as long as the action continues and the spark of opportunity can be fanned into a flame and perhaps into a roaring furnace of achievement, the overachiever is the man least likely to leave. He is not the type of man who is constantly talking to executive head-hunters, reassessing his market value, or dithering as do so many low achievers.

Johnny is a delightful, procedure-knowing, wench-chasing, competent middle manager who could be excellent if he concentrated, but whose greatest achievement in fact is managing to stay employed at all. Nevertheless, every couple of years he announces solemnly and "in the utmost confidence" to his friends that he is now thinking seriously of resigning and starting a new career in earnest. Most of his friends, the first time they hear the story, go to a great deal of trouble to recommend him as a good potential employee.

On one such occasion Johnny was invited to at least four interviews for important jobs and, because he is intelligent and personable, he landed three excellent job offers. To his friend's surprise, and annoyance, he turned down each one of them. Later his friend discovered that Johnny had done the same thing with several other people, telling them each the story of wanting to start afresh, swearing each to maximum security, and leading each to suggest him for a top position. However, each time he landed an offer he turned it down. What he wanted was reassurance, not action. A true overachiever would be capable of providing his own reassurance.

Another acquaintance, let me call him Charlie, talked of wanting "to get things moving." "The company is wedded to inaction. So I decided to leave," he explained to his uncle, a successful executive.

By coincidence it was only two days later that the uncle heard of a position as a vice president of an especially dynamic consumer-goods company. He recommended Charlie most warmly for the position, thinking truly that he was a good man.

The following afternoon the potential employer called the uncle in considerable annoyance.

"Damn it, what sort of a lazy idiot did you recommend to me?"

"What happened?" the uncle asked in surprise.

"After your recommendation I called Charlie and asked him to drop into my office. I told him that you had recommended him very highly and that I was most interested in seeing him. I also told him that we were in a hurry to fill the job."

"Right, so you mentioned to me; and so I told him, too."

"He said he'd drop in in about three weeks' time—after his vacation!"

Charlie wanted to know his value—not to demonstrate it!

The overachiever who leaves one job nearly always finds another, and often a better one, quickly. He does so because his track record is generally impressive and, importantly, because he works with such determination at being reemployed.

One man, having left his job through sheer frustration, answered an advertisement for a marketing position in a cigarette company. A few minutes after his interview started, however, it became clear that he was overqualified for the marketing job.

"You also have a top sales opening," he said: he must have done a great deal of digging to discover that information. "Here is my sales resumé," he continued with a grin. "I thought it might come in handy!"

Of course he got the job.

Most men, however, walk into their initial interview totally unprepared. Although the literature on finding a job repeatedly stresses the necessity of researching the company you are interviewing—and although it is simple enough to go to any reasonable library and look up in Dun and Bradstreet, Moodys, or the trade journals all you need to know about the company—surprisingly few men bother with this effort. Two or three hours' study lets you make the sort of impression during the interview that will almost guarantee you a job. Yet there are men who have been out of work for months who have never even set foot in a library. These are the men who may have the ability but lack the drive to find a new job.

One man with a good track record at a giant consumer-goods company approached Candy Corporation of America to apply for the job of vice president of marketing. He appeared to have done his homework and he made a good impression. Thinking that he looked like a good potential candidate, the company's personnel man started to "sell" him on the company: he told him of the spirit of the executives and how they often worked late into the night to beat out their plans together; he described how the whole staff of the company was dedicated to growth and how even the president's secretary once sold a carload of candy when they desperately needed the sales. Finally, convinced that he had explained fully, he asked for questions.
"What is your vacation policy?" the man wanted to know.

Contrast this with Michael Rosselot, who wanted to join the same company because he had read that it was run by action people.
"You are the one company for whom I intend to work," he announced. "I'll take any job that puts me inside the door." He then explained why in considerable detail, demonstrating how much he knew about the company. He was hired even though initially there was no real job for him. He was simply too good to miss.

Perhaps the most unfortunate reason for which an overachiever may lose his job is success; that is, when he has succeeded so well in building the organization for which he works that it becomes a prime target to be gobbled up by a larger company. When it is sold, too often the purchaser cannot come to terms with the previous builder—and out he goes! Even if he stays, he faces a dilemma. Wishing to be loyal to the acquiring company, he feels he should no longer create the same sort of unilateral action he did before the acquisition. Instead, he marks time; and the new management wonders how such a slow, procrastinating executive has built such a reputation so fast.

Myles Mace and George Montgomery, Jr., describe a typical case in a little book called *Management Problems of Corporate Acquisition:* A company president, used to action, whose company was acquired, felt that now for the first time he had to leave it to the head office to tell him what to do. It was a terribly depressing period for him because the head office was silent, busy, and unwilling to make long-distance decisions. Finally, with things going from bad to worse, a confrontation was inevitable. "Why didn't he take the initiative and just move, keeping his superiors informed as he went along?" the acquiring company's president wanted to know rather angrily.

The attitude of action, the spirit of achievement may lead a man to quit through frustration; or, occasionally, may result in his being fired. But it is the same spirit that gives him the resiliency, the tenacity, and the drive to become reemployed where he can achieve even more. Fortunately for the overachiever—and for the whole business community—overachievers not only achieve, they bounce!

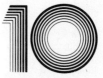

Motivating
the Overachiever:
Measuring the Achievement

Money is the traditional reward for all business achievement and, although there are significant differences between the monetary rewards obtained in varying professions, a persuasive argument can be made that within any one profession, the amount of money earned is almost directly proportional to the level of achievement. Thus, while it is true that clergymen earn far less than do doctors or lawyers, it is equally true that, just as senior partners in law firms earn more than juniors, so bishops earn more than curates (although it remains to be seen whether the correlation between achievement and ultimate promotion is quite as clear!).

Nevertheless, many people no longer work exclusively or even primarily for what money can buy. While they are re-warded in relation to their achievement, they are not motivated in relation to their reward. As Arthur Koestler says, "If Archimedes was originally motivated by the desire to obtain money or favors from the tyrant of Syracuse, his jubilant shout was certainly not due to anticipation of the reward."

When you have enough of the necessities and don't really get much advantage from more money per se, then further financial success becomes the measure and symbol of your success rather than an entity worth striving for in its own right. If you lack that understanding, you may "drop out," become a playboy, or in some other way deviate from what our society considers acceptable behavior. Even though men do not work for wealth alone, it would certainly be a mistake to discount the tremendous advantages that wealth brings to the overachiever. The first and most obvious is convenience which, near its peak, is luxury, and ultimately opulence.

Bill Eberle, the former president of American Standard, former Speaker of the Idaho House of Representatives and former senior adviser to President Nixon on international trade, is quite a success. I had just returned from a conference held in Aspen, Colorado, when I met Bill, who was just back from Paris. He told me that he loved Aspen and owned a condominium there; he also told me he had a condominium in Paris and one in the Caribbean and one . . . He stopped when he saw my surprise.

"We collect condominiums," he said by way of explanation.

If you ever doubt how pleasantly money allows the successful man to live, just drive for a few hours through the "back country" or Belle Haven area of Greenwich, Connecticut, or the Shaker Heights district of Cleveland, or the Indian Hills suburb of Cincinnati; they are lovely areas. But if you want to swaddle yourself in their luxury and you have no inheritance (and you married a poor girl for happiness), then achievement of at least some degree is essential.

The second advantage of money is that it provides a desirable degree of freedom of choice. Money buys the time to do things that are considered subjectively to be desirable—at least partly because they are not *requirements* for living. They may, seen objectively, indeed be "work"; but they are desirable to their doer because for him they are relaxation. He can concentrate on the things he enjoys doing and in which he has become specialized while paying someone else to clean the drains.

It is clear then that money is not the sole motivating factor in the business world. The freedom to make choices is a force in its own right. But a far more powerful drive is the instinctive drive for prestige; this urge has been a factor since the very earliest eons of life. It is a drive that may have provided the pressure for those "wandering fingers of green [that] crept upward along the meanderings of river systems and fringed the gravels of forgotton lakes," which Loren Eiseley imagines endless geological epochs ago, as slowly the world changed from "vast drifts of stone and gravel, the sands of wandering wastes, the blackness of naked basalt, the yellow dust of endlessly moving storms" into the life-seething world we know today. Whether our pre-ancestry was driven by such instincts or not, there can be no doubt that virtually all animal life experiences an instinctive drive for status that in many instances may be more powerful than the drive for life itself. Man is no exception.

Part of this instinct is the instinct for survival, the instinct for space, the instinct for what Robert Ardrey in *African Genesis* calls the "territorial imperative." But the instinct exists just as strongly where there is no imperative for territory, where food supply is abundant and where available space is virtually unlimited. It is an excess of this drive and this hunger for territory, transmogrified to a drive for dominance, which characterizes the overachiever. He wants above all to be the leader, he wants to be admired. "We have a preference," writes Arthur Koestler in *The Anatomy of Snobbery,* "for people who are likely to leave their imprint on our time. Whether they leave their imprint as politicians, Chinese scholars, or collectors of snuff boxes does not matter . . . to be one's self is not enough; one must be 'somebody.' "

A member of the board of directors of a three-billion-dollar company, who is also president of a giant financial institution and who sits solid and wise on the boards of several other enormous concerns—a man who could retire to his cattle ranch or play billiards or sit with his feet relaxed on an ottoman viewing whatever scenery in the world took his fancy—chooses instead to work, emerging from one difficult meeting only to rush to the next. I asked him one day, as we were both hurtling down in an elevator from the thirtieth story of a New York skyscraper, "Why?" It was with a twinkle in his old eyes and with real delight that he said to me, "It's not the fact that I'm a director which pleases me. It's that I've reached the stage in life where they hold the board meetings only on days convenient to my schedule!"

Perhaps it's just as well that so many men with enormous achievement potential choose to use their drive and their ability to make things happen in the business world—and choose to measure their success by the amount of money they make—for other forms of advancement in the pecking order might turn out to be very antisocial indeed. John Maynard Keynes, in *The General Theory of Employment, Interest, and Money,* wrote:

> *Dangerous human proclivities can be canalized into comparatively harmless channels by the existence of opportunities for money-making and private wealth, which, if they cannot be satisfied in this way, may find their outlet in cruelty, the reckless pursuit of personal power and authority, and other forms of self-aggrandizement. It is better that a man should tyrannize over his bank balance than over his fellow citizens.*

Money is "the root of all evil" only to those who lack it. To the overachiever it has become—and, I think, fortunately—the measure of success and, to a large extent, the measure of personal value. Prestige and power have been the end of achievement since man's genesis—and long, long before.

Money, the modern world's most specific version of evolution's concept of territory, and power are two strong forces motivating the overachiever. They are not, however, the only forces. Necessity, that is, survival, remains one of the primary instincts. Together with its symptom, fear, it may be the greatest motivator of all. There can hardly be debate that fear—and in the business world many fears, such as the fear of failure, for example, abound—is a fantastic motivator. If you read the quiet desperation of Walter Morris in his *Journal of a Discarded Man,* you will feel that fear most acutely: fear of rejection, fear of unemployment, fear of the worthlessness of self, fear of being truly discarded—the fear that Morris calls being "out in the field of Hazard." More important perhaps than any other fear is the motivating effect of the fear of what "other people" may think.

"A large part of civilized man's environment is made up of other men, whose fears, hopes, beliefs, prejudices, and values exert a great effect in determining the content of his mind," writes F.S.A. Doran. On the face of it, the content of the over-achiever's mind will be less determined by what others think. His confidence in his own ability is such that he is usually confident that his peers will ultimately understand and admire. Yet for the overachiever necessity is a drive just as strong as for the normal man, for it may be the manifestation of an inner need and insecurity. Some writers have gone so far as to suggest, as did Chester Burger in his rather aggressive book, *Executives Under Fire,* that such men as Riklis of Rapid American Corporation, General MacArthur, Zeckendorf at his prime, men who most of us would consider to be archetypal overachievers, were "compulsively driven men." He hints that their drive comes from "deep inner self doubts." He states quite blatantly that "because many of these men are, not so far beneath the surface, intensely insecure men, they have fashioned elaborate devices to assert their dominance in the hope that this will make them secure." I believe Burger makes a small point anyway. There *is* a type of inner necessity that drives the overachiever, but I doubt that such drive could be called insecurity; to suggest that most achievement is merely a compensation for insecurity seems improbable. A man is said to be strong and confident if he does strong things. I question the value of a theory that also portrays such strength as a symptom of insecurity (and presumably insecurity as the ultimate expression of self-confidence and inner strength!).

Money or territory; freedom of choice; prestige; power; "what others think"; real or inner necessity . . . what more could motivate an overachiever? I believe there is one further force motivating businessmen: the insatiable desire for immortality. From the builders of the pyramids to the lowest worker who calls his son not John Smith but John Smith, Jr., this has been a wholly human striving, an ambition apparently unknown to any creature but man. At its most obvious level it led a Charles Revson, while he was the largest shareholder and absolute dictator of the Revlon Cosmetic Company, to have installed in the Lincoln Center for the Performing Arts in New York, a fountain inscribed with the immortal words: "Placed in honor of Charles Revson by the Charles Revson Foundation." At another level lie the many university endowments made with the sole stipulation that the buildings they finance must perpetuate the name of the donor.

A most laudable method of self-perpetuation is to help other people. The great philanthropist is remembered first individually, then in folklore and, finally, perhaps even in history. The success of many a worthy Quaker in the business world—the Rowntrees and Cadburys who came to dominate the chocolate business in England, to name just two—may well be a drive to this sort of immortality. The post-business careers of the Rockefellers, the Kennedys, and their ilk can certainly be viewed as nothing more or less than the building of social pyramids which, even if they do not last quite as long as those in Egypt, have a great deal more vitality while they do.

On a more complicated level, the desire of the overachiever to get things done may also partly be pyramid-building. Obviously, the other factors we have discussed all form part of his drive to action. But his desire to be immortalized probably plays an important role. (Indeed, this desire for permanent achievement may be one of the reasons that big companies, which offer perpetuation of achievement to a greater degree than do any small ones, can attract high-caliber overachievers even if they offer them less income and less freedom of action.) Such men, in creating movement, establish their achievement in two ways: they achieve the end result of what they seek to do; but they also create what Louis C. Schroeter has called "organizational élan." It is a term he borrows from the French philosopher Henri Bergson, who developed the phrase "élan vital" or the "compelling desire which exists within the individual to improve or effect change." Schroeter points out that the leader of an organization plays the decisive role in establishing this élan. But he does not mention the important fact that, once established, this élan may become a corporate tradition that may live on well beyond the life of its creator.

These then are the fundamental drives which motivate the overachiever, or indeed any man in business. The question is: How are these achievement-motivators tapped?

We have to determine the preconditions that must exist before motivation occurs. So much has been written about this that it may seem both presumptuous and implausible when I suggest that there are really only three prerequisites to mobilizing the basic motivators—and that all the literature boils down to only those three. Although many thoughtful and scholarly writers on business topics would disagree with me, nevertheless, I stand basically unmoved, not because I can always argue successfully with the experts on theoretical grounds, but because my views have proved to be of some usefulness over a number of years in their practical application in the business world. Thus, with only limited hesitation and apology, let me say that I believe that in one way or another, all techniques of business motivation require the establishment of the following three preconditions:

1. The establishment of a group of people, a team, which will serve as the overachiever's "extended arm" *and which is dedicated to achievement, not simply to cohesion.* It must be a team that not only works well together, but that really *works*—rather than talks. Unfortunately, teams said to "work well" together very often do not work at all; they merely enjoy each other's company! Almost always, to achieve action in a team it is essential first to achieve effectiveness in at least one individual. It is the overachiever who is usually the key to the team, the catalyst who makes sure it keeps producing. While the existence of a functioning team is a requisite for the motivation of the overachiever—who will become hopelessly frustrated if forced to rely exclusively on his own human and therefore limited resources—it is equally true that the team will remain at best a group of friendly but ineffective colleagues until an over-

achiever is pushed into or emerges in its midst.

2. The establishment of an environment of challenge, for without challenge, people fade. As usual, Peter Drucker has said it completely:

> *The young knowledge worker whose job is too small to challenge and test his abilities either leaves or declines rapidly into premature middle age, soured, cynical, unproductive. Executives everywhere complain that many young men with fire in their bellies turn soon into burned-out sticks. They have only themselves to blame: They quenched the fire by making the young man's job too small.*

3. The establishment of an environment where dealing well with people or, in my terms, persuading them tactfully, is rewarded; the establishment, in other words, of an atmosphere where there exists a real desire to motivate people. Surely this prerequisite is so obvious as to be virtually a self-defining necessity in motivating anyone.

You may ask how reams of literature may be written to expand on those three simple requirements. I think the reason is that once you have established the requirements for motivation, you may have established very little. Certainly, you have not motivated anyone, for you may place a man in a position full of élan, create about him an atmosphere of challenge, encourage him to motivate himself and others—and yet he may fall asleep either metaphorically or even physically within five minutes. The question the literature is really tackling is: Once you have established the right circumstances for motivation, how do you take the step that rouses the man to enthusiasm?

In my view, the answer to this question is a condensation of the three prerequisites I have mentioned into one simple principle. I believe that the desire to achieve (whether it is merely a summary of other pressures, or is itself the cause of overachievement) provides the key to motivating overachievers in business.

The problem of how to motivate them boils down not to long theoretical discussions of what turns men on, but rather to a determination to challenge men. *To motivate overachievers you must organize your business so as to give achievement recognition!* How to *do* this is perhaps more complicated.

The most obvious definition of an effective executive (i.e., one whose achievements should be recognized) is that he is an executive who makes effective decisions. Unfortunately, the definition is only useful where effectiveness in a decision is measurable as an objective fact. If the decision deals in areas where there are well-established, achievement-oriented ways of measuring the effect of the decision, then the effectiveness of the executive can thereby be measured. For men whose achievements are so large in relation to the size of the organization for which they are performed that they cannot be overlooked or seriously mis-assessed, the measurement of effectiveness is not a major difficulty. But in organizations where many decisions appear to be matters of consensus, or on junior levels of management where the results of decisions are largely indefinable, the problem is far greater. How does a man know whether he is effective? How, for instance, can you show the achievement of a product manager or a salesman when it depends largely upon outside factors? Is the man who survived in Argentina during the 1973 plague of kidnapings but who failed that year to introduce any new products for his company more or less effective than the man who, in the economic explosion in Brazil the same year, was able to increase sales of his new products at only the same 10 percent that the gross national product grew?

There is no simple effectiveness measurement possible in these—and in most—business circumstances. Yet it is axiomatic that you cannot motivate a man to be effective unless you can show him the results of his own efforts and thus encourage him to ever greater achievement. It is difficult, I think, for a young overachiever in a large company even to know whether his achievements are being recognized. Generally speaking, large companies are effective at differentiating the good people from the bad. Usually there are carefully honed policies of evaluation in which every employee of any potential merit at all is evaluated not only by his immediate superior but by a group of independent executives able to observe him. These evaluations are generally carefully investigated whenever any opportunity for advancement within the corporation occurs. Unfortunately, sometimes it is also true that this evaluative procedure is not adequately explained to the junior employees. In particular, the young man who is doing well tends to be ignored. Since there is nothing that has to be said to him to improve his operation, we tend to say nothing, while a word of encouragement could be of great value.

Nevertheless, although personal encouragement and reassurance help, objective self-evaluation, where the employee can see for himself how well he is doing as measured against objective factual criteria, is a much more effective tool of motivation. In my view, the whole answer to motivation in business may be summarized in the phrase, "measurement of results." The man who can measure his performance will be motivated to improve it. If he is not motivated by that, I doubt whether he will be moved by anything on earth!

There are two principles involved in adequate measurement: the first principle is that the accounting function must be so organized that wherever possible the manager has the illusion of profit control—and hence the illusion of what I call "achievement control." The best way to do this is to establish an accounting technique in which all variables not connected with the project in question have been kept equal. Thus, any achievement that shows up in the figures must relate directly to the credit of the manager of the project. Let us take the case of a brand manager. He must be given some figures to be elated or sad about. Since he is a human being he must be able to measure his achievements objectively and then be emotionally responsive to the success or failure shown by those figures. The problem is that a brand manager of, say, five years' experience can hardly be expected to appreciate all the factors making up the profit picture of a major company for which he works. Therefore, the best measurement device of his effectiveness may be, for example, the measurement of sales; he understands and can see them clearly. More importantly, he can directly affect them by his own efforts.

Even where the brand manager is told that he has profit responsibility, it is usually no more than an illusion since he is not given full business responsibility.

For example, at Procter and Gamble, one of the cradles of the brand manager system, profit is assigned per case sold. The first case sold is said to make exactly the same amount of profit as the last case sold; and a case sold in January is said to make exactly the same profit as one sold in June. In other words, profit is *solely* related to sales. In the real world, myriad factors affect real profit. But the Procter and Gamble brand manager—and for that matter most brand managers of limited experience—can have no real understanding of how these factors relate to profit. He has an *illusion* of profit responsibility but he has not the vaguest idea what his actions actually do to profits.

Many companies are faced with a dilemma. One horn of it is that to do the best for the company the manager, in this example the brand manager, must be given a simple measurement device against which to assess his own achievement. The other horn is that a young brand manager, no matter how dynamic and creative he may be, cannot possibly master all aspects of business sufficiently so as to have profit-control or even real-profit understanding. Therefore, true profit very often cannot be used as the criterion for measurement. Yet in the long run profit is the only really valid criterion for achievement in business. Fortunately, it is possible to take giant steps towards avoiding this dilemma. One company did it in two ways:

First, they hired the right people. This is easier said than done; good people are always hard to find, because everyone is trying to find them. In this case, they succeeded only because they recognized that the marketing manager with the broad business experience necessary to understand profit is a much more valuable entity than is an ordinary brand manager.

Second, they trained their marketing people in the "principles of profits" so that even if they didn't know by *how much* certain factors would increase or decrease profits, they nevertheless understood almost instinctively *whether their actions would have a positive or negative effect* upon the profitability of the company. Even though they measured their effectiveness in terms of sales, they were not in danger of achieving sales in an unprofitable manner.

While it may be very difficult to teach a man the specific effects of his actions in profit terms, it is relatively easy to tell him which type of actions will have generally positive or generally negative effects. The principles of profit deal with the *direction* the act he undertakes causes his profits to move in rather than with the specific amounts of profit or loss that will result. It is a happy truism that if every action makes profit, then total company profits will inevitably improve through constant, widespread action. How many organizations can boast that their marketing men get ulcers every time they take an action which directionally reduces profit?

The concept of the principles of profit is a thoroughly practical and useful one in many businesses. It is, therefore, worth summarizing here. There are six principles of profit:

1. *The selling price must be more than the combination of variable costs of raw materials, packaging materials, labor, and so on, plus fixed manufacturing overhead, plus variable costs of selling, including freight and warehousing, plus variable costs of sales promotion and advertising, plus fixed administrative costs, plus profit.*

A truism, perhaps. But if it is a truism that selling price has to be above the variable costs of the product plus a fair allocation of the fixed costs, then it is a truism that is often disregarded. I doubt whether the marketing people and sales people in one company in twenty are provided with enough information on the profit breakdown of each brand to be able to set prices on the basis of that knowledge. I doubt whether one company in fifty can honestly claim that it is willing to discontinue a big seller if it fails to cover all costs plus profit. But I do not doubt for a moment that many marketing men have never really considered the implications of this first and fundamental principle of profit.

Naturally, however, there are certain exceptions to this first principle. These fall under the second principle:

2. *Products can be sold below full costs plus overhead and profit contribution, provided that they do not in any way reduce the sale of products that do cover their full costs and contributions.* If the factory is working at 75 percent capacity and the sales department is unable to sell the remaining 25 percent capacity at full price, then selling the remaining capacity at a reduced price may be sound business. The first 75 percent of the business has covered all of the fixed overhead. Therefore, provided the additional business covers more than its variable costs, it follows that an increase in total corporate profitability results.

This principle of profit is probably the most difficult of them all to live with amicably. Nine times out of ten a product developed only to cover a portion of the overhead ends up being a main part of the business. Soon its sales volume is so high that it is given priority over more profitable brands. It displaces more profitable brands but fails to contribute as much as did the displaced brands to the overhead; and it leaves the company, in total, less profitable than it was before.

A newly acquired company sold four hundred items. On inspection by the new owners, it turned out that fully two hundred were selling at below full, variable, and fixed expenses. None of these items had any profit even planned for it. There was a prompt inquiry by the new owners!

It turned out that each one of the unprofitable items sold by the company had been introduced with the conviction that it would add to the total sales of the corporation. Admittedly, each item would not cover its full costs, but since overheads were already covered by the basic line, that was not considered necessary. The old management was certain that each item would, in fact, raise total profitability. The fallacy in this thinking (and in the vast majority of other, similar instances I have observed) was that the introduction of each marginal item in fact did cut into the sale of a full-profit staple item. The reasons for this were numerous.

In some cases, the marginal product took up sales department time that could have been better spent selling the basic line. In others the cheap product took up research and development time, so that the basic line's quality deteriorated. In yet others, the less expensive line simply drove out the similar but more expensive product because the buyer refused to buy expensively when he could buy inexpensively. And there were many other reasons. But in each case, the result was the same: a product originally introduced to be an "extra" item that did not have to make a full profit became a staple item—but an unprofitable one. And profits declined.

The danger of violation of the second principle of profit can be overcome only if management insists that items sold at less than full profit be approved by the executive committee or some similar group. Generally, this committee should give approval to such "contributors to overhead" only if they are *completely* noncompetitive with existing brands. A candy company making another candy product, however different in formulation, is making a competitive product. But if it markets a cough drop— or it makes a candy for sale in a foreign country in which it is not represented—it is indeed making a product which is completely noncompetitive with its business.

3. *The creative process and the profit-making process tend to be incompatible; but the profit motive must be given preference.* Only the very best copywriters, package designers, or artists do not think that talking about money and expenses in connection with their work is a violation of their "artistic integrity." Moreover, many marketing- and advertising-agency executives feel that worrying about money when it comes to the creative process is a mistake. They frequently believe that if you do worry about money while looking at things "creative," you will usually end up paying $20,000 for a poor T.V. commercial instead of $30,000 for a good one.

Of course that would be false economy. In truth, considering the cost of television time, it is false economy to run an ineffective commercial whatever its price. But the answer is not to spend $30,000, but to spend $20,000—and get a good commercial at that price. After all, when you ask your factory manager to cut costs, you don't ask him to ruin the product! I am convinced that saving money is as practical—and as difficult—in the creative process as it is everywhere else.

However, many a full-blooded, creative "genius" will throw a temper tantrum the moment you even mention costs. Since business needs such people, the answer is to disassociate the creative and business aspects of the job. Let the creative man not worry about anything as demeaning as money! But let the marketing man worry a lot about the money and, if necessary, let him sufficiently modify the project after it is completed by the creative man so as to reduce its price while maintaining its quality.

4. *Profits are made only by men who have learned to be both penny-wise and pound-wise.* The companies that have hit hard times because of waste in small things may well number more than those that have found themselves in trouble from doing the small things right but the big things wrong. The marketing manager must watch the million-dollar advertising budgets. But he must also watch the paper clips!

5. *Money invested costs money—and generally the more invested the greater the rate of interest per dollar.* What this means is that the first million dollars may cost you prime interest rate. The second million dollars, prime interest plus 1 percent. The third million may be almost impossible to get and, therefore, may cost you the exorbitant interest rates charged by certain factoring companies. The last million dollars, however, will cost your soul; and there is no level of return on investment that will pay for that.

The point is not academic. Marketing men again and again evidence dismay that management has turned down their suggestions, failing to understand that the best business proposition and the highest return on investment becomes untenable if there is not sufficient money available to pay for it.

6. *Having too many people in an organization represents far and away the greatest cost to any business.* Parkinson's Law is well known. But it may not be quite as well known that the cost of the incremental people brought into an organization multiplies *more* than geometrically with the number of such extra people brought in.

One marketing man in a medium-sized company can do, let us say, 75 percent of what needs to be done. Two men can do, let us say, 80 percent of what needs to be done. (You will note that the second man, if he is paid the same as the first, is already fifteen times more costly per unit of work than the first.) The addition of two or three more people to try to achieve that last 20 percent of what is necessary to do the job is probably the "straw" that forces the company to set up a marketing department; then it needs a department head, an assistant, two more secretaries, and a set of new procedures. Moreover, an organization of six or seven men —assuming the rare circumstance that they are all dynamic and open minded and have excellent communication—*may* be able to do as much as 80 percent of the job. Those extra men have contributed nothing—at high cost.

But the worst is yet to come. Now the company hires twenty more people to tackle that last, elusive, 20 percent. With each man they add, they also add more problems of communication, more internal politics, more compromises, more red tape and misunderstandings, more wasted effort, and in general, more impediments to progress. Each additional man costs not only his salary and fringes, but adds also a certain amount of harm.

The question is, how much is enough? After all, it would hardly be feasible to run General Motors with just one man. The answer is, in rule-of-thumb terms, that hiring additional people to assist management is valuable only in two circumstances:

a. If the new employee has the capacity to do a job that no one in the company has the time or the skill to handle. This means that a request for a new assistant cannot be phrased as it normally is: "I need an assistant to help me." Rather the request has to state: "I need an assistant to do the following specific tasks . . ."

b. If the new employee is being hired to be trained to replace an existing employee.

If these simple criteria were applied to all hirings, most companies would operate more effectively and with lower costs.

The second principle of measurement is that where "quasi-profit" measurement is simply impossible, it is essential to establish other nonprofit-oriented standards of achievement. Not all jobs at the middle-management level of a major corporation—indeed not many of them—can realistically be measured in profit terms or even in terms that give the illusion of profits. Fortunately, there are many ways in which such nonprofit-oriented achievement standards can be established. The important matter is to establish a standard which is numerical and which can be self-assessed by the man to be motivated. How to do this depends on the type of job and company.

One company uses the number of new products placed into test market as its measurement of achievement.

Another, although it would not admit to anything so foolish, does in fact use the number of hours a man works as such a measurement. Although this fulfills the criteria of self-assessment and numeration, it fails to satisfy the criterion of common sense. As a measurement it has no usefulness other than to prove that an ill-thought-out measurement is less use than no measurement at all.

A third company uses a complicated system of savings and efficiencies as the measurement.

All measurement techniques have tremendous potential disadvantages and must, therefore, be used with the utmost caution. Equating sales with profits places too much emphasis on sales—which may turn out to be unprofitable.

The company mentioned earlier that had over two hundred products that did not contribute full fixed and variable expenses also had nine products that actually cost more in variable cost to make than their selling price. The reason for this incredible state of affairs was that sales as a measurement of achievement had got out of hand: sales had become the *sole* measurement.

Similarly, all the other types of achievement measurement can, if allowed to, expand to extremes and become worse than useless, resulting ultimately in the attainment, with tremendous difficulty, of undesirable goals.

The obvious conclusion is that goals must be multiple and carefully controlled.

Colgate–Palmolive is one of the finest companies I know in the establishment of simple, clearly defined, and easily measurable multiple-goal criteria. They encompass: sales expansion; productivity increases; rises in sales per employee; cost reduction; inventory and accounts receivable (working capital) decreases; and, of course, profitability improvement—all in simple-to-understand form. They work brilliantly, and it is no coincidence that the company has expanded dramatically in the last few years since such self-assessable goals were established.

Problems of
the Overachiever:
Larger Than Life

The overachiever, while he is more energetic, more curious, more determined, may also be prone to more trouble than the ordinary man. And his troubles are likely to be just as varied and original—and just as oversized—as are his achievements!

A most incredible piece of trouble happened many years ago to an unusually honest young man who is now enormously successful. In those days he was a junior employee in a large corporation. As it turned out he was, in fact, doing extraordinarily well, but no one had bothered to mention that fact to him. Looking at him today, as he sits near the top of a substantial company, looked up to by his peers, admired by his subordinates, courted by his competitors, and loved by his superiors, it is difficult to imagine how he could ever have doubted his own ability. Nevertheless, it is true that he had become, as he himself describes it, almost traumatized with the idea that he was not progressing as fast as he should. He compensated, as an overachiever will, by working harder and harder and achieving more and more. Still no one told him how well he was doing.

One day, late in the evening, in his office, he found he needed a fact book and, as was the normal routine, went to his boss's office where the fact book was kept in a special cabinet with a dozen other such books full of the minutiae of the company's consumer-goods business. It was quite customary for juniors to walk into the office and borrow whichever book they needed. He walked in, thinking of nothing in particular but the task at hand, when right in front of him, so obtrusive that he nearly collided with it, was a desk drawer left open; and on the top of it, more seductive than was ever a siren's call, he could clearly see a personnel-evaluation file—with his name on it!

Man of action that he was—and is today—his hands flew to the folder and opened the cover. In this case his instinct for action lead him astray.

"Brilliant," "Needs to be promoted," "Great potential," said the file. He closed it rapidly, flattered but realizing that he should not have opened it.

But a cleaning woman had seen him and reported him. The next day, quite inevitably because of the way that big companies must work, he was fired!

The problems of the overachiever certainly are varied and original. But let me make it clear that I am not talking here about problems such as the desire to move forward too rapidly, the difficulty the overachiever has in containing his ambition, the tendency to be disruptive. The subject of this chapter is the kind of problem that goes to the essence of what the overachiever is. These are the problems that may, on occasion—quite frequently, in fact, for the man who is able to overachieve only by the use of his last ounce of ability—slow down and ultimately destroy the overachiever's ability to get anything done at all. They include the problems of rank bad luck such as falling into a debilitating illness; but more frequently, they are self-induced. Whether or not they can be overcome is really a question for the psychologist; but I suspect that a great deal can be done to overcome even the most substantial of the overachiever's problems if only he will recognize them for the real barriers they are.

There is, I believe, a clear pattern to the types of trouble to which successful men fall prey. Indeed, the pattern is widely recognized among all businessmen. It is simply that because the overachiever is such a strong, "wave-making" fellow, the waves made by his problems tend to be tidal.

There are said to be some nine million adults in the United States who are either alcoholics or problem drinkers. Admittedly, such statistics are not clear in their definition, but the exact figure is in any case unimportant, for there can be no doubt that alcohol is a major burden to a very large number of people. I am not suggesting that businessmen are more prone to alcoholism than are men in other professions; as far as I know, there are no statistics which would suggest this. I am suggesting, however, that alcohol represents a major problem in the life of many people in many walks of life; and that for a man who is highly active and influential at least partly because he is running near his optimum capacity, a reduction in that capacity by even a small amount may be of serious consequence. Alcohol causes such a reduction.

Philip was a heavy "social drinker" who would occasionally get creatively "smashed." Once during a party he burned his clothes, starting with his socks and working up gradually until decency forced the host to douse the fire! Everyone ignored these lapses. They added spice to their parties; they were a little wicked; they were fun.

But slowly his career seemed to decelerate. Where promotions had been rapid, they came only occasionally. Where new products in his charge had been successful, they now seemed dogged by bad luck. Where there had been a spirit of enthusiasm in his department, there seemed now to be a pervasive, nagging boredom. It took some time, but eventually he quit his job, no one knew whether by desire or by suggestion. The new job he took at first seemed like a major step forward, but that feeling lasted only a few months. Soon he started complaining that he could get nothing done. That "they" were always after him, that he lacked freedom. It was not long before he left, citing a "management disagreement." Philip is now a "consultant" making a meager living by selling his past abilities to his past friends. He never gets "smashed" anymore or goes on drunken flings. He is no longer "fun" but rather the soul of propriety—but he relaxes with four or five Martinis every evening of his life.

A brilliant young investment banker with whom I worked some years ago was one of the most lucid men I have ever known. I always felt we worked together perfectly. He was a joy to negotiate with even when he was on the other side, for his clarity and intellect made dealings easier—although he was a tough opponent! One day, however, the deal I was making, this time with my friend as my ally, almost fell through because he became totally confused. I had no idea why. We were forced to break up the meeting. When we reconvened the next day, my friend looked tired but was otherwise normal. I quite forgot the incident.

Within a few months, however, my friend the banker disappeared from the scene. The deal had long been consummated and I lost contact. It was not until a year after that I heard to my horror that he had committed suicide.

"Oh, didn't you know?" a mutual friend exclaimed when I asked him why. "He was a hopeless alcoholic."

Another of the more prevalent downfalls of the overachiever is that he burns himself out. This is normally a phenomenon of the fairly young, for if a man is able to survive and continue to achieve beyond middle age, it is unlikely that his energy will evaporate until it does so for reasons of old age or disease.

Jack was one of nine children born to the wife of an unskilled laborer in the slums of Chicago. With that background it would have been an amazing achievement to become educated and attend *any* university. Jack was able to work his way through the Harvard Business School.

When he graduated from Harvard he joined a group of his friends and opened a small grocery store. Within just a few years they had parlayed this one store into a small chain. He sold out when he was still in his late twenties because he found that the donkey work of the grocery business had become unendurable. Instead, he joined a major consumer-goods company, rose within its ranks, and before the age of thirty-five was national sales manager of a three-hundred-man sales force. He led it with dynamism and determination. His career was assured; he was on his way to glory.

Suddenly he stopped. Instead of leading his men to ever higher sales records, as he used to do, he started writing detailed accounts of why sales were not improving; instead of flying overnight and meeting a salesman for breakfast, he would fly during the day and have dinner with old friends; instead of watching like a hawk for unjustified exaggerations in salesmen's expense accounts, he would exaggerate his own. Finally, in exasperation, his boss decided to talk to him.

"Do you feel your performance is up to standard? Do you feel you are progressing as fast as you should? Are you satisfied?" his boss asked.

"Yes," the former overachiever replied. "I have done very well. I am completely satisfied!"

Closely akin to the burning-out phenomenon is what I assume Dr. Laurence Peter would probably call "Petering out." The Peter Principle, as everyone now knows, says that men are usually promoted up to their level of incompetence. It is true, of course, that overachievers have incompetence levels just as do other men. They are rather high, but they are reached rather quickly since the overachiever's career outpaces that of his more normal rival.

In the case of the overachiever, however, the situation may be substantially worse than in the case of the normal businessman. The overachiever may have so much career momentum behind him that he may be able to crash through his first level of incompetence onto a new level so far beyond his ability as to make it seem as if he is almost criminally negligent.

Harry Schonfeldt had impeccable qualifications: at college, he had been president of the student council, president of his fraternity, a football player, and to round it off, a Phi Beta Kappa. He was also an affable and good-looking fellow. The company he decided to join felt fortunate to have attracted him and gave him a special sales-training position.

A few months after he joined, the position of district sales manager became available and, since he seemed to be doing so well already, management decided to take a chance and give young Schonfeldt the job. The gamble paid off elegantly. He was superb. His energy, good humor, and innate ability more than made up for his lack of experience.

Six months later the firm became interested in an acquisition. In order to decide whether to proceed, a detailed acquisition study was needed. The president of the company decided Harry could handle the job and again Harry earned accolades. His native enthusiasm and pleasant manner never left him, and his intelligence was more than sufficient. His report was so well-prepared that, when it was decided to proceed with the acquisition, the president decided to place Harry in charge of the acquisition negotiations. He realized, of course, that Harry had no experience in this kind of activity. But then, had he not mastered other jobs in no time in spite of experience lacks? He was an out-standing man; he would do an outstanding job. In any case, the rest of the executive staff was too busy with even more important activities.

When the acquisition eventually fell through everyone was, of course, disap-pointed. But such matters often go wrong. Many acquisitions that start out looking excellent break down somewhere along the way. The president was not upset with Harry Schonfeldt's performance. Instead of moving him back into sales, he promoted him to head the new venture group. It was as director of this group that he did such a spectacularly awful job that he was eventually asked to resign!

A few days later, while lunching with one of the lawyers who had been involved in the acquisition attempt, the president happened to relate the whole unfortunate story.

"Why would you have promoted the young man after he did such a lousy job on that acquisition?" the lawyer asked.

"Oh, he didn't do a bad job," the president said. "I know we didn't manage to acquire the company but that really wasn't his fault, was it?"

"Oh yes it was!" said the lawyer with great conviction.

Harry Schonfeldt had reached his level of incompetence without anyone noticing. Instead they pushed him from his first level right into a second level where no one could remain in any doubt.

Closely akin to the phenomenon of petering out is the phe-nomenon of growing too fast. They are similar but not identical. Petering out leads one into a position one is incapable of han-dling, whereas the supergrowth syndrome has the young busi-nessman fail in a job he would have been capable of doing had he sufficient experience. In other words, he has reached his position too early in his career.

A bright, overachieving young man (with the most spectacular shock of golden hair about which he was immensely vain) joined a large consumer-goods company as an assistant product manager. Instead of taking the normal year to learn the basics of that position, his obvious talent resulted in his becoming the administrative assistant to a vice president after only three months. The position was normally a sort of male-secretary-without-typing job. But the young man parlayed it into a position in which he was of great personal help to the vice president. He attended most of the important meetings and read all the mail. Soon he seemed to have learned a great deal more about what was going on in the division than one would have expected in such a junior employee. Quickly he was promoted to a line job in a small overseas subsidiary. Partly as a result of the people he knew back at head office through whom he could expedite a great deal of his work, and partly because he was truly a competent man, he continued to look first class.

It became clear, however, that he was lacking in fundamental training, and the decision was made to take him out of the small overseas subsidiary and put him back for one year into head office, to give him the basic marketing training he had missed. This move was to be preparatory to promoting him to director of marketing in one of the corporation's large subsidiaries—and from there to the moon!

A few days before he was told of these plans he resigned from the company and accepted a job as director of marketing with a major competitor. The move was such a promotion that he could not be dissuaded from leaving. He would not listen to the view that he lacked the experience needed. He took the job —and quite predictably within a few months he failed dismally.

The story has a happy sequel: he recognized that what had been said to him about his lack of training was true and he decided to retrench his career. He joined another major corporation in a junior marketing position, to get the basic knowledge he lacked. Today, some years later, he is well-trained and very successful.

The world of business is getting more complicated at an accelerating rate, as are the worlds of science or economics or history. The advent of the computer has added a deluge of facts, far more than we are capable of assimilating. The growth of the population, and its wealth, have added an enormous number of new consumers; technology has added a wealth of totally new products. On the other hand, shortages, repeated energy crises, every type of pollution, and the increase in the demands of human life have added a series of new problems as infinite as the opportunities with which they coexist. An increasingly frequent phenomenon in the business world is the man who has the capacity to keep up with his business but is overwhelmed by the difficulty of keeping up with the world. Change is simply too much for him. Leonard E. Strahl, in his book *Moving Business,* talks of the "fearful ramifications" of change. While the statistics suggest that we are becoming healthier physically and that by the end of the century our average life span will exceed one hundred years, the statistics on mental health seem to be less optimistic. Partly, of course, this is because we are defining psychological and mental disease more clearly and therefore including in the group some suffering people who were previously considered healthy but "odd." Partly, however, I suspect these discouraging statistics are the result of the complication of life. And the complication of business life, being just as great, leads sometimes to breakdown in the capacity of the overachiever. He moves up until, not because of incompetence, but because of his lack of resiliency, he can simply no longer keep up with the killing array of figures and facts and alternatives and decisions.

"I am astounded that there are so many problems to be solved every day in the business world," "Ranger" Hamilton complained.

"Ranger" is Dr. Eleanor Hamilton, a leading marriage counselor and author of numerous books. She is a fascinating woman who has turned her attention to a tiny tropical island in the Caribbean Sea called Dominica, where singlehandedly she is creating a cottage industry, introducing birth control, and trying to improve the lot of the natives of this Eden. Suddenly she has become a businesswoman who is, in her words, "trying to make Paradise into a nice place to live."

"How do you businessmen manage to deal with so many different problems every day? Sometimes it's personnel, sometimes it's supply shortages, sometimes it's a change in the value of international money, sometimes it's import restrictions, sometimes it's legal difficulties, sometimes it's packaging, sometimes it's buying, sometimes it's selling. How do you men do that without going half-crazy and simply throwing up your hands in despair?" she asked me.

Some men resolve their difficulties by limiting themselves to specific pieces of administrative work. Others, the overachievers, take on themselves ever increasing problems. Sometimes, if they have enough resiliency or if they do not feel the pressure just as a racing driver does not feel the normal fear of high speeds, they are able to achieve more and more and ultimately become overachievers of renown. But there are other times when they reach a point where the weight of change is too great. Then they either cease trying to achieve or, in occasional tragic cases, they crack under the strain.

When a somewhat aging businessman finds himself at last at the power pinnacle, he suddenly finds too that he is once again attractive. The most gracious, beautiful, and attractive women find him interesting. Naturally, he is both gratified and tremendously flattered. In the first two or three decades of his career he was probably married and dedicating his time, energy, and enthusiasms toward achievement. Suddenly in his forties or fifties he finds himself adulated. Brilliant and beautiful, sometimes even stunning women seek him out. They may take up a great deal of his time.

The situation of the overachiever outdistancing his mate is another common problem.

Charles was a simple engineer when he married Helen, an air hostess he met en route to Grand Rapids. For a few years his travels continued to be local and she was a great asset to him in the cities they visited together: places like Cedar Falls, Iowa; Moosejaw, Saskatchewan; and Charleston, Virginia. Undoubtedly part of Charles's upward progress in his company had to do with Helen.

Today, however, as a result of that progress, he no longer visits provincial American towns. Instead he negotiates huge engineering contracts with dictators in Latin America, legendary sheiks in the Middle East and shipping tycoons in Greece. But his little Helen can launch no thousand ships, nor even one!

Less often, but not infrequently, it is the women overachievers who outdistance their men.

Shirley was a housewife five years ago; today she is a major and highly controversial figure in the world of business and education. But Jim, her husband, is still the regional sales manager he used to be, both in fact and in outlook. "I want to be a sales manager," he tells his friends. "I expect to be that until the day that I retire. Then I want to go to Florida and I already have my apartment picked out in the town where I want to live. I can't understand why Shirley is so dissatisfied with that life. We have everything planned. We have everything the way we always wanted it."

"The way *he* always wanted it," Shirley explains.

Fortunately, even though most overachievers face all the problems I have outlined above—alcohol (and perhaps other drugs); burning out; petering out and its related phenomenon, growing too fast; being overwhelmed by change; getting mixed up in the "fast-woman syndrome"; outgrowing his mate; and perhaps many more—most overachievers overcome them. The hunger for success is so great in some men that they are able to overcome even the worst difficulties.

A senior executive in an important advertising agency, who was rising dynamically to the top, suffered, at the age of thirty-nine, a massive stroke. He became totally paralyzed for several months, and finally recovered only sufficiently to sit in a wheel chair, lift a telephone with his left arm, and talk, more or less coherently, out of the left side of his mouth. He can neither move out of his wheel chair nor even dress himself. Yet today he has built a thriving business sending out samples through various special techniques. He makes more money and has a more important business position than he ever enjoyed before. He is, of course, the exception. But then so is every overachiever.

There is one major danger for the overachiever from which recovery is difficult indeed: it is the occasional tendency to exceed the bounds of morality—or even legality—in the desire to get something done.

Robert Vesco surely is a man who had the drive, the intelligence, the innate ability to be an overachiever. Moreover, he started his career most effectively, building a strong and apparently worthy company under him. It was only in taking over the mortally wounded OIS Corporation from Bernard Cornfeld that he seemed to exceed the bounds of propriety. In doing so he sunk to a position where his energy is now devoted to fighting legal battles for his own protection. Even if he avoids prison and saves some of his money by remaining in Costa Rica, it is highly unlikely that he will now ever make any real achievement.

The movie called *Save the Tiger,* released in 1974, shows Jack Lemmon as Harry Stoner, a man who, in his rush to achieve, cuts corners—practically all the corners one can imagine. He pimps for clients; lives beyond his means in a Beverly Hills mansion; fixes the books of his corporation, and evades taxes. Finally, he arranges for a rather successful warehouse fire. But in all of this he has lost his reason for achievement. Only the habit is left. And the habit is not sufficient to create real achievement; it is enough merely to maintain the momentum to go from bad to worse.

The reason for this tendency to fall from grace into immorality is, I suspect, largely the arrogance that stems from overachievement itself; it is an easy trap to fall into. For the overachiever can demonstrate his superiority over other men on an almost daily basis. His houses grow faster than do his peers', his "castles" are larger, his success is palpably greater. It becomes all too easy for him to think of himself as being above the restrictions of lesser men, and hard for him to fight the Nietzschean "Superman" concept. As Shaw has his successful businessman, Undershaft, put it in *Major Barbara*: "Be off with you, my boy, and play with your caucuses and leading articles and historic parties and great leaders and burning questions and the rest of your good toys. *I* am going back to my counting-house to pay the piper and call the tune." Undershaft, it has always seemed to me, had an arrogance barely matched by Shaw's own.

Few overachievers are able initially to view their attainments and then remember the exhortation of Ecclesiasticus: "The greater you are, the humbler you must be." But I do believe that eventually the overachiever does learn to put his own talent into the context of what *could* be done and not of what other men do. Then truly, in a world which has such infinite need for improvement, even his greatest achievements seem paltry. No longer can he say with Frank Lloyd Wright, "I, having nothing to be humble about . . ." Instead he must dedicate himself wholly toward achievement in order to insure that, in the panoramic canvas of the evolution of mankind, his own tiny step forward has any significance at all.

It seems to me that the overachiever's greatest danger is to forget his reason for wanting to achieve and become a man without a dream, struggling without a purpose. It is a danger that occurs particularly when a man reaches middle age and finds that his career path and his probable future achievements are already predictable. He knows that in the absence of bad luck, he will attain his ambition. Worse, he realizes that the chances of his achieving a greater success than he can foresee are remote.

It is men who face this "ambition realized" block who switch wives or, for the wrong reasons, start new careers. The phenomenon of the forty-year-old who suddenly comes home and says to his wife, "I quit my job today. I'm going to be a writer" is well known. The man who dumps his charming, sophisticated, and attractive wife of twenty years to play around with some pretty "chick" is even more usual. Not as clearly recognized, but I suspect far more common, is the man who loses the ambition to do anything at all and continues to go to the office not because he is driven by the desire to achieve, but because he sees no alternative.

Back in 1955 Herbert Mayes, who had for twenty-five years been Editor of *Good Housekeeping* magazine, said in a speech to the executives of General Foods: "After twenty-five years of work, with scarcely a lazy minute in the lot, I am able to lay claim only to the small and uninspiring total of three hundred issues of a magazine . . . a lifetime of labor, and only twelve magazines a year, for twenty-five years!" Since he was a brilliant man introduced for that speech by Roy Whittier, who had been Chairman of the Plans Board of Young and Rubicam Advertising Agency and a senior marketing executive at General Foods, as "a visionary and a realist, a poet and a pragmatist, a combination of vivid imagination and sound business judgment," he might have felt disheartened with his achievement. Fortunately, he was, as Whittier said, a man of sound pragmatic perspective. He was, moreover, actually an overachiever of considerable merit who did as much as anyone to create *Good Housekeeping* and with it affect, I believe positively, the life style of millions of people throughout the world. He was, I think, correct when he concluded his presentation to General Foods by explaining that his life and his work had been "consequential and satisfying." I believe the lives of overachievers are.

Most overachievers survive the middle-age trauma I have described as they survive other traumas and problems in their lives: by action.

The overachiever may expand his business opportunities by moving to a new job or a more challenging aspect of the old one.

A woman who was manager of a chain of retail stores decided that even though her company was expanding satisfactorily, it could grow much faster. When the board of directors refused to give her the opportunity to accelerate, she decided to buy the company. It took her almost ten years of frantic efforts to find the money and persuade the existing owners to sell. But she did eventually, and when she did, she built the sales not by the traditional 8 or 10 percent a year, but by 100 percent a year for the first five years she owned the corporation. She had been a disgruntled forty-year-old when she started the fight. She was an exultant fifty-year-old when she won it. And at fifty-five she was very rich and successful indeed.

The overachiever may extend his personal growth by using his typically large income to buy the leisure necessary to study some new aspect of his life.

One man, without reducing his dedication to his business, started re-educating himself to understand the emotional and "feeling" part of his life. The same Dr. Eleanor Hamilton I mentioned earlier runs a counseling center in an enchanting forest house in Sheffield, Massachusetts, called the Hamilton Center for Family Life. This man expanded his emotional response to his wife and his children and enhanced his own emotional completeness by enrolling himself in the Hamilton Center and participating with several others in an exploration of the sensitivity of his body and soul. His business in no way suffered; it was in fact considerably enhanced because he added to his already great competence a degree of sensitivity to people he had previously lacked.

The overachiever always fights problems, including the problems of lethargy and boredom, with action.

Some very extraordinary and determined men, those who are lucky and effective enough to reach the pinnacle of achievement in their chosen field while they are still young, actually start out on an entirely new career.

". . . the curtain is being raised all over the nation on new . . . and very often exciting second acts," writes Damon Stetson, in *Starting Over*, ". . . both men and women are turning to second careers . . . are taking the plunge and beginning another way of life in their middle years. And there appears to be no limit on just where the leap will take them."

Charles Percy went from business into politics with considerable success.

Robert McNamara, who saved Ford, went into government and became the most successful Secretary of Defense, in the opinion of many, that the United States has ever known.

Aristotle Onassis, starting as a poor young man of questionable ethics, built a fortune in the business world and in building it greatly strengthened the economy of Greece. It was only near the end of his career that he decided to start on a new one: the career of socialite. The acquisition of the Casino in Monaco and his marriage to Jacqueline Kennedy surely made him one of the most successful career socialites ever to exist.

Jack Dreyfus, one of Wall Street's leading financiers, abruptly retired in 1970 at the age of fifty-six to devote his time and considerable energy to working with a rather obscure drug, Dilantin, which he believed had some broad, long-range medical benefits for mankind.

The greatest challenge that faces any overachiever is to know what to do when he finally reaches the goal he has been hungering for. The magnitude of this problem depends partly of course on the age at which the man reaches this goal. Even the most dynamic man eventually slows down. If he has had as his lifelong ambition the determination to build a thriving community in the Arizona desert and he does this by the time he is sixty-five years old, it may be that he will be happy for the rest of his life, retiring there and enjoying the proceeds of his labor. But many men reach their goals before they tire. Frequently they start something as exciting as their original task, but very different.

There are many alternatives at every time in life. The young man about to graduate from college no longer must ask himself what sort of job he should seek, but rather what sort of a life he wishes to lead and what sort of a contribution he intends to make. The fantastic variety of choice is such that he can no longer ask himself merely "Where do I want to work?" or even "What do I want to do?" as did his father. Instead, he must start by asking "Who am I now and what do I want to become?"

The question by no means applies only to the young. Life decisions can now be made repeatedly *throughout* life. They are very difficult decisions, particularly for the overachiever, because successful men are so strongly tied-in financially to the positions they hold. "The restrictions that present themselves as benefits," Drucker calls them. Corporations, determined to hold onto their best people, create what are known as "golden handcuffs"—plans whereby the executive, if he stays with the company, will be reimbursed some very large amount of money, often, at senior corporate levels, millions of dollars. If he leaves, he forfeits it all. It is not easy to decide whether to accept wealth plus dissatisfaction or even boredom, or to continue to struggle financially—and subject your family to those struggles—in order to obtain personal satisfaction. It is easy to say that satisfaction is all and that we live only one life, but the constant rededication to striving, to the expansion of personal horizons, is not a rededication that all men can or wish to make. "Change is not made without inconvenience, even from worse to better," writes Dr. Johnson, but for once he understates. The difficulty of making changes is enormous, for all human beings. Even though change has been recognized as inevitable ever since Heraclitus said, "There is nothing permanent but change," it is rarely other than traumatic. Men hate making decisions and when those decisions are easy not to make it becomes most tempting to avoid them.

The greatest of all achievements is to be an overachiever in unrelated fields in one lifetime. This is the sort of ambition that requires almost ascetic dedication. It is the sort of ambition only a true overachiever could even harbor. Its implementation is very rare.

However, there is a common—and thoroughly undesirable—type of dual activity, although hardly dual achievement, which occurs when a man is frustrated in his job and unable to make progress. Bored, frustrated, hurt perhaps by the lack of recognition, he may decide that instead of continuing to strive within his regular employment, he will work only the minimum amount needed to entitle him to his salary, and then use his energies and abilities to make his achievement outside his business life.

This is a terrible solution. Not only are his talents thereby lost to his regular employer, but worse, no one else really benefits much from them either. For any man, even if he works in the most superficial way, uses up the best of himself during each day from nine to five. When he returns home at six he must be either tired from the effort he placed into an exacting and challenging job—or bored to lethargy. He will then be more likely to watch television than do anything else. Even if he arouses himself from an unchallenging day's stupor, he is most unlikely to be able to achieve much. Almost always, if a man seeks to gain his satisfaction outside the area to which he is forced to devote the majority of his time, he becomes an underachiever.

A very average manager of the market-research department of a medium-sized company is, in his spare time, mayor of a town of 100,000. While he is fascinated by politics, and I am sure potentially very good at it, he doesn't have the time to do this second job right.

A tired old journeyman executive in direct-mail advertising amazed me the other day when he told me that he had been the captain of a battleship in World War II. I was the more surprised when he said that in his spare time he was curator of a small war-history museum.

"If only I had time to run the museum right," he lamented. And I lamented with him.

The solution is to motivate men in their primary jobs. True, if these men were really overachievers they would motivate themselves. But if they are not, then their potential may very possibly be far greater than their actual achievement. This potential must be unleashed by the overachiever; the man who himself wants to achieve must find the way to turn on the resources of these others and capitalize upon their real abilities. *The best way for the overachiever to extend his own achievements is to use the leverage the abilities of other men provide for him.*

What Attracts
the Overachiever

There are business situations that particularly attract and excite the kind of man who wants to create action. Industries in which people are bright and competitive and where events move fast attract more than their proportionate share of overachievers. But surprisingly, dull industries are not always eschewed by the overachiever; sometimes he sees in them an opportunity for moving more rapidly through the vacuum of inaction than would be possible in an organization where fast action is already the norm and where acceleration would be difficult. I find it tempting to suggest a somewhat paradoxical general rule: the overachiever is attracted most to companies where the action level is either exceptionally high or exceptionally low. As we shall see, there is some truth to this rule, but the exceptions are too many and widespread for it to hold up well. Therefore, we shall conclude that there is no general rule, but that it is the circumstance of the company which creates the attraction—or causes the barrier—for the overachiever.

The railroad industry contains at least its fair share of poorly run businesses. It is bound up in a morass of legal maneuverings. Many of the companies in the industry are in, or on the verge of bankruptcy although they often continue to operate unimproved and unabashed. Many railroad executives seem to be more interested in the *status quo* and the maintenance of their incomes than in trying to run their organizations properly. Yet despite this situation, the railroad industry has also attracted some of the brightest and toughest of entrepreneurs who, like Alan Boyd of Illinois Gulf Railroad, have risen above the difficulties and built or maintained huge and profitable companies. The average standard of railroad executives may not be as high as that of the men who abound in, for example, the consumer-goods industries; but even a business as underachieving as the railroad business in the United States does manage to attract *some* overachievers—there are such worlds for them to conquer!

In industries manufacturing such products as soaps and detergents, where Colgate–Palmolive, Procter and Gamble, and Lever Bros. fight with such vigor that products constantly improve, prices are constantly kept at the lowest possible level, and the ultimate victor invariably is the consumer; or in foods, where much the same thing applies in the battle of General Foods, General Mills, Ralston Purina, Quaker, Hunt–Wesson, and many others; or in the automobile industry where such a competitive battle rages that the public is guaranteed the most technically advanced products at the lowest prices; or in toiletries and pharmaceuticals, where dozens of firms compete to the benefit of consumers throughout the world; the men who are attracted to fight the "battles" are generally bright, driving, and competitive. These are the kinds of industries which attract more than their fair share of overachievers.

The phenomenon of the dynamic business attracting dynamic men is, I believe, an excellent example of the attractiveness of action. There is magnetic appeal to an industry in which competition is intense. Just as the best soldiers gravitate to the toughest fighting, so the dynamic businessman gravitates to those companies where action is hottest. Perhaps it is because to succeed against brilliant people is a far sweeter achievement than to succeed against the dull.

On the other hand, there are industries that on the face of it, would seem to be attractive only to the business hack, but which attract at least their share of overachievers. The retail business, long-houred and boring as it is, would hardly seem likely to attract a bright young mover. Why would he be interested in becoming a store manager in some slightly downtrodden supermarket chain? Yet, while there are few Harvard Business School graduates operating as managers of your local A & P, the retail business has attracted some overachievers of mighty proportions. The men who founded The Great Atlantic & Pacific Tea Company still cast a Colossus of Rhodes shadow over the entire retailing business of the world. Similarly, banking, with its low pay, conservative outlook and "banking hours," is an area that logically should attract less than its share of the young overachievers. Perhaps it does attract less than do other fields, but there can be no doubt that it attracts some. There is one ambitious young woman, for example, in the heart of one of the most staid of the banks in downtown New York, who by some intangible magic seems to create action undreamed of in that bank before.

Since it is not possible to determine in principle that certain categories of business attract overachievers, my conclusion is that every industry can—and the fundamental tenet of this book is that every industry must—attract some movers and doers. It is only the clearly moribund industries that attract none; and I am convinced that that is a main reason they *are* moribund.

The question is not what types of industries but rather what types of companies and situations are capable of attracting the overachiever. It is a question which every business and every businessman must answer effectively for survival.

The first attraction is the attraction of like for like. One overachiever usually attracts another.

When Townsend joined Avis he attracted, or unearthed, a wonderful team of movers who "tried harder"—not, I suspect, because they were Number Two, but because they thought that their boss and they themselves were Number One.

When the Rugby International and sports hero of Dublin, Tony O'Reilly, joined Heinz and became first its president in England and ultimately its president and chief executive officer world-wide, he pulled with him a team of overachieving fighters who reactivated the Heinz Corporation.

Overachievement in organizations tends to be self-perpetuating. The chief executive officer, if he is eager for action, will hire department heads as eager as he to move forward fast. They in turn will naturally choose the sort of men who love action. All the way down the line good men will hire others in their own image, until the company has such a reputation for action and energy that the overachievers fight to enter.

The second and closely parallel attraction of certain companies for the overachiever is what one might call the "fun of the battle." It is in these companies that it is possible to see young executives "stand like greyhounds in the slips, straining upon the start." Young men want to test their mettle against others, and particularly against those they admire.

Colgate–Palmolive, which is quite remarkable for its will to achieve, has fewer hacks, and, by no coincidence, fewer people per sales dollar than most companies of its size in its general field. In 1973 *Fortune* magazine placed it number 65 in sales, but number 91 in number of people employed. (Today, after further growth and acquisitions, it would be higher in sales, but lower in people per sales dollar.) I believe that this relatively low manpower-level is, as much as anything, the reason that the Colgate desire for achievement is so advanced.

Action is effected more easily if the man who wills it has only one or two others to convince—and greatly hampered if, before any action can be achieved, he has to convince a multitude of middle managers.

Competition is a most valuable motive force in industry. On the other hand, it takes some wisdom to harness it so that it does not get out of hand. There is a potential danger in fostering competition between strong men: they may waste some of their energy on infighting instead of working single-mindedly toward the corporate purpose. Even where this danger is eliminated (as it can easily be by management attention) there is another problem that is more difficult to forestall: the danger of seeking perfection. Trying to do things too well may be akin to not getting them done at all. "The greatest enemy of good is best."

The classic example of trying to reach perfection and instead achieving almost perfect disaster is the case history of the Edsel automobile. This was to be the Ford Company's greatest achievement. It failed because each portion of it was so refined and rerefined, so overdeveloped in name, appearance, and marketing detail, so market researched, polished, and discussed, that when it was all together it became something approaching a monstrosity: a huge car combining all the vulgarisms of automobile design thought of up to then. Worse, it entered a market that was being evangelized by Romney and his compacts and that was embarrassed at being reminded of last year's crass patterns of consumption.

Dr. Eleanor Hamilton believes that the demand for perfection in one's partner is one of the greatest destroyers of love. It is one of her five destructive "riders of the apocalypse." The example may be extreme but the principle applies to organizations. As Browning put it, "What's come to perfection perishes." The drive for perfection, as distinct from quality in business can be a destructive force; it may be fostered by too much competition.

It is for this reason that even though they love competition, sometimes overachievers prefer to enter underachieving situations where their pursuit of action will stand out dramatically. This is an excellent approach if they do not so rock the staid corporate existence that they achieve merely the disquietude of the incumbent management—and their own removal!

Since this approach is valid (particularly for the young man gifted with a certain degree of innate tact), it is worth examining the various ways in which overachievers may enter successfully into underachieving situations.

One approach is to join a small, often family-owned company and build it to glory. The most important criterion for choosing such a company is that the owning family allow the newcomer enough latitude to put his own ideas across and move forward. Nothing is less productive than jettisoning the old approach without completely replacing it with the new one. If that happens the company inevitably operates with the worst of both alternatives.

A large American company had just opened a branch in Germany and hired a number of brilliant young Germans straight out of university as product managers. They were highly intelligent and educated, but they had little experience in marketing and none in the way that American corporations operate.

Each morning, when the American director of marketing walked into the office, the young men would stand rigidly to attention, click their heels loudly, and in the harsh tones normally reserved for military command, would fire at him the words: "*Guten Morgen,* Herr Goodwin!" He was embarrassed.

"I would really appreciate it," he said one day to one of the young men, "if you would be good enough to call me by my first name, Harold, and relax a little. After all, this is an American company and it is normal in American companies to use first names."

"*Jawohl,* Herr Goodwin!"

He tried on several further occasions to persuade them to call him Harold but to no avail. Eventually he was forced to resort to the Germanic way of doing things.

"You will all call me Harold from now on. I want no exceptions," he ordered harshly. "And don't click your heels either."

"*Jawohl,* Harold!" came the unison response. And there was no click in the room.

The next morning the president and chief executive officer of the enormous American parent concern was scheduled to visit his new little subsidiary in Germany. He was a dignified, white-haired gentleman of about sixty years of age to whom deference by subordinates had become as normal as the air he breathed. As he got out of the elevator he happened to pass by a young man, hardly more than a boy, who had worked for the great corporations's German subsidiary for no more than two weeks. During that time the young man had learned only one thing, namely that "Herr Goodwin" had told him that in American companies one always uses the first name. He didn't understand why, but that was the rule. Because he was German, he would stick undeviatingly to the rule.

So, as the great captain of industry emerged from the elevator, the young man turned sharply toward him, remembered in the nick of time not to click his heels, summoned up his total command of English, and uttered with determination the words, "Good morning, Sam."

The removal of existing cultural or business *modus operandi* may be entirely valid and desirable; but it can be successful only when it is immediately and completely replaced by a new set of guidelines. In the business of running a business, falling between two stools is always uncomfortable and usually results in a painful bump.

A not infrequent approach to eliminating the control of the incumbent family is to acquire the firm outright. This is the venture-capital approach I spoke of in an earlier chapter. It has frequently been successful, but it carries with it its own enormous problems.

One first-class businessman trained in a large business decided to run a pencil company. He did quite well, but found himself on a treadmill of insufficient capital. Forced to factor his receivables, that is, to borrow money using receivables as collateral, and thus constantly having his company and its receivables under scrutiny, he found that his flexibility was so reduced that he had practically no opportunity to implement the new plans with which he wanted to rebuild the company. Determined to move forward anyway, he started to implement his own procedures but never got them completed. Bump he went between two stools.

Another chose garden furniture as his venture arena. He quickly acquired two companies, but then became embroiled in a proxy battle for control of the new holding company. As a result, he started to increase the distribution channels, which was his plan for building the businesses, but then, with his mind distracted, ended with a garden furniture company that sold to a limited number of outlets but financed a sales organization large enough to service every outlet in the country. The seat upon which he thought he was firmly astride split, amoeba-like, into two stools. And again, bump!

Yet a third overachiever managed to raise the funds to take over a typesetting firm, determined to make typesetting kits for the retail market as an educational toy. In the midst of the expansion into his new plan, he found that the members of the family—who had agreed to continue to run the basic business—became so outraged at all the changes that they left. Suddenly, the family's contacts stopped buying and the company's basic business, which paid the overhead and was to finance the expansion, dried up. Instead of running a consumer-goods business, the young man was forced to become an old-fashioned typesetting salesman. He didn't do badly because he switched entirely to the old stool, but he never really fulfilled his dream. Had he tried, he too would have landed painfully between the old and the new.

Generally, the success of men who move into such small companies is, to put it generously, mixed. They frequently find that their determination to action, their sophisticated business outlook, their impatience with the incumbents' way of doing things is too severe. They try to change things too fast. Over-rocking the boat, they frequently almost sink it.

One $15 million company prepared all its invoices by hand, obviously an unsatisfactory technique. A bright young manager had just been appointed. She took one long look at the situation and decided on action.

"Computerize," she ordered.

They came to her with a variety of reasons why it wasn't possible. But it clearly was possible and clearly right, so again she said: "Computerize." Computerize they did.

In the process it was inevitable that some people had to leave. After all, the purpose of the computer was to replace the old-fashioned hand preparation of the invoices and thus run the business with fewer people. Among the people who left was Molly, the invoice checker, who had been with the company forever.

Almost immediately everything went wrong. Orders were returned. Quantities were incorrect. Shipments arrived on the wrong days and the invoicing was a disaster. The young woman investigated her computer and grilled her computer experts, searching for the center of the problem.

"The data we are feeding from the old hand-kept tabs into the computer is wrong," one computer expert explained. "No computer can possibly do a better job than the data it is fed."

"Garbage in, garbage out!" said another, more succinctly.

"Then how did we manage to get all the invoicing right when we did it by hand?" the young woman asked. "After all, we didn't make those mistakes and we were operating off the same data."

"Molly always put us right," one of the invoice clerks said.

Someone else chimed in, "We always asked Molly."

Molly, it became known, had a phenomenal memory, and even though the customer cards, the data from which had been carefully punched into the new computer, were out of date and wrong, it didn't matter because Molly made the corrections out of her head.

There are many instances where dynamic overachievers take family businesses, turn them around, and ultimately achieve success. The annals of business are loaded with such stories. But they are far fewer than the failures. Where this approach has been successful it has been because the entrepreneurs involved were overachievers of quite extraordinary capacity or overwhelming good luck.

For the man not interested in trying to take over a small business, an alternative is to join a large and lethargic company in order to get things moving again. This is a tremendous job because the lethargy of such organizations can be fantastic. Just as, at their best, large business organizations can change the world, so at their worst, it takes almost the strength of the world to change them.

The continuing failure of some tough and tenacious executives to turn around the A & P Company is a case in point. Regularly, the top management of the organization has expressed the determination to make it aggressive and up to date. But several A & P buying offices still require the salesman to stand in a cubicle on one side of a waist-high table and talk to the buyer across the flat surface as he stands on the other side. It is hardly an atmosphere that persuades employees or visitors that the firm now has an aggressive and modern spirit. Yet many of the A & P executives are potentially among the most effective in the country.

It is an enormous job to change the religion and breathe verve into a big but tired corporation. But it is not impossible.

Bob and Larry Tisch acquired the Lorillard Company in 1970 when its share of the cigarette business had been declining in a gentlemanly sort of way for years. It was a thoroughly charming, anachronistic, country club.

Bob ran it and, being the owner, had a greater chance to make changes than he would have had as an employee, even as an employed president. Nevertheless, the transformation of Lorillard was remarkable. With the help of such men as Lester Pollock, his tough, energetic, financial man, Bob Tisch and the new president he appointed about a year after he acquired the company turned around good old Lorillard and made it into a competitive, action-oriented, profitable, and growing business. It can be done, but it is very difficult.

A new sales manager was placed in charge of a tired, discouraged, seventy-five-man sales organization serving the toilet-article subsidiary of a large conglomerate. No one had cared for this small company; no one had visited the salesmen in the field and given them the encouragement most sales people need from time to time; all the company's employees were dispirited. Worse, the former sales manager had announced the previous year that salesmen's cars would have to be painted yellow and white. "So that we know where you guys in the field are."

The new manager did little more in his first two weeks than send a personal, handwritten letter to every salesman and cancel the policy about the garish, taxi-like cars. Sales for the quarter rose 25 percent.

At the end of his first year, the new manager, who by then had established strong rapport with all his men, bought seventy-five small-model cars and had them painted yellow and white. He sent one to each salesman as a "memento." From that day on, the salesmen became a fighting unit ready to take on the competitive world and win. The symbol of their team spirit, voluntarily established, became this: any man who exceeded his sales quota earned the right to have his car painted bright yellow and white!

The overachiever knows he wants action. He seeks it in many places: where it already exists in abundance; where it hardly exists, but is likely to be welcomed; and, paradoxically, where it is abjectly absent. But always, he enters a situation where he is convinced that there is a crying need for himself.

To be successful, industry must attract the overachiever. To attract him, industry must recognize how vitally he is needed.

Overachievement:
A Sense of Purpose

There seem to be two general assumptions underlying all the behavioral sciences: that human behavior is largely predictable (even though we may not yet possess the means of prediction); and that shortcomings of the brain are, in principle, rectifiable. It follows that the ability to predict carries with it the implication that modification and hence substantial improvement of the brain is possible. I share the hope that this is so. But it seems to me that hard evidence has yet to be gathered. The premises remain unproven. Certainly, B.F. Skinner and many others have demonstrated fairly conclusively that certain specific and elementary behavioral patterns can be induced, modified, or eliminated. That humans can be trained as can dogs has long been known. But whether this means that the use of conditioning techniques will be able to produce any type of behavior desired —let alone produce a utopian society—is open to a great deal of questioning.

There is no doubt, too, that character can be modified by drugs and by operations, as long as we work at fairly elementary levels of specific behavior. Indeed, behavior can obviously be changed by persuasion alone. "It is not cynical," writes Perry

London, "to say that the systematic persuasion methods which are psychotherapy are salesmanship elevated to the level of technology." But whether the over-all human character can be changed, whether a dull man can be made to scintillate, an impetuous man given wisdom, or an ineffective man taught how to achieve, remains to be demonstrated. If the hope for such improvements is realized by the psychologists—or by the invention of behavior pills as simple as aspirin or even by the development of an operation as painless as that my barber performs upon my hair—then, in my view, the great advance will not be in rectifying the psychological shortcomings in man; rather, it will be in allowing all men to achieve up to their full potential. Then overachievement will be the norm, and perhaps our world will have taken one further massive evolutionary stride in the direction of its ultimate destiny of enormous failure or fantastic success.

However, for the time being—even in a world where the laboratory creation of life seems within grasp, where cloning is written about in the popular press as if the creation of limitless numbers of identical beings is something we can expect to see within the lifetime of our highly differentiated children, and where organ transplants are commonplace—the overachiever cannot be artificially developed.

At the extreme of our teaching techniques, limited, innate capacities for overachievement may be so heightened that they may *seem* to have been developed from nothing, just as the hearing of the almost deaf can be so improved by a hearing aid as to seem to be miraculous cure. This is why the overachiever warrants writing about. But the fact remains that he can neither be neatly summarized like the formula for sulphuric acid, nor, in spite of occasional, sleight-of-hand, near miracles, can he be created.

We have gone as far as is now possible with considering who the overachiever is, what constitutes his special drives, and how they can be recognized and enhanced. There still remains the question: Why?

A friend of mine indulges in a piece of cocktail-party banter by suggesting that an entire theory of life can be built on the assumption that man is better than the amoeba.

"If you believe that man is no better than the amoeba, I can do nothing with you," he explains to his hostess. "But if you will grant me that man is better than the amoeba, in other words that there has been spotty but distinct forward motion over the evolution of the past two hundred million years, then you must logically agree with me that the most advanced of men are the best. They are at the apex of evolution; they have progressed or evolved the furthest distance from the amoeba. Further, you must also logically agree with me that any reactionary movement, any back-to-the-woods naturalism, any move toward conservation for its own sake, as distinct from conservation for the sake of further advancement to civilization, is counter to the good of the world."

While the hostess goggles, and her husband from across the room sees the necessity of rescue looming, my friend continues with the final thrust. "So turn up your air conditioning and close the windows. Admire the world from within man's cocoon of civilization and forget once and for all about the beauties of nature—they are merely relics of the past!" It is banter, of course, and my friend is not serious. But banter with a point. Banter not easily forgotten.

Thoreau, lionized as the father of "back to nature," is misunderstood by all such cocktail-party hostesses. He did not say that he went back to nature at Walden, but rather that he sought to advance into the mind, moving forward from mere lust for luxury in order "to live deliberately, to front only the essential facts of life, and see if I could not learn what it had to teach . . . to live deep and suck out the marrow of life." There is nothing evolutionarily regressive about trying to expand the mind!

Many men have been awed by the possibility that out of the ooze from which, through an immense series of evolutionary circumstances, men eventually emerged, there may yet rise new and greater creatures. It is possible—and perhaps even desirable—that mankind's current evolutionary pinnacle may be superseded so that our innate weaknesses no longer limit our upward struggle. But it is more immediate and much more exciting —and above all more *useful*—to think of the continuing growth of man as the everlasting evolutionary path.

Man today is in the middle of a fantastically rapid advance; the statistics of our progress are almost overwhelming. The changes in man's knowledge, his technology, his social conscience, his physical exploration, his interstellar search, his very psyche, are so incredible that each of us moves further and faster every year than did decades and possibly centuries of our forefathers. So rapid is our advance that it seems to me conceivable that we are actually able to observe, as on those rare occasions when it rains in a desert and the cactus flowers open with visible motion, the movement of evolution.

Was there ever another such time? Perhaps the years the ice-age glacier moved in so close as to block out the sun; perhaps when the first fish learned to breathe air; perhaps the moment when some giant comet crashed into our earth and jarred out a new mutation in our evolution? Even if we can perceive that we live in a time of evolutionary lightning, we cannot tell where or how that lightning will strike. To ask to know which path evolution will take is to beg the fates too demandingly.

But living must continue and we must develop a practical approach to life. To lead the most useful life may well mean to approach the matter of daily living on the assumption that an evolutionary branch of great value—and, who knows, ultimately of the real essence of future development—is the one in which both you and I, as reader and writer, exist. It is on this admittedly self-centered, self-serving, and highly shaky platform that my particular evaluation of the importance of achievement rests. But it is a platform where a platform was essential. I have found no other of comparable utility.

Achievement makes life worth living, not because of the luxuries it brings—for it is possible to live happily without those— but because it brings a deeper and more basic satisfaction. Achievement provides the meaning that, I think, is essential to the enjoyment of a fulfilled life. Perhaps only in the mainstream of evolution is such satisfaction possible. Perhaps satisfaction is the instinctive feeling of the stream pushing us forward, further and further from the amoeba. In *Walden,* Thoreau writes:

> *I know of no more encouraging fact, than the unquestionable ability of man to elevate his life by a conscious endeavor. It is something to be able to paint a particular picture, or to carve a statue, and so to make a few objects beautiful; but it is far more glorious to carve and paint the very atmosphere and medium through which we look, which morally we can do. To affect the quality of the day, that is the highest of arts. Every man is tasked to make his life, even in its details, worthy of the contemplation of his most elevated and critical hour.*

For this sort of achievement, everything, every sacrifice, is worthwhile. If achievement is sufficient to make life meaningful, then sacrifice to that end is not sacrifice at all but joyful giving. Then, in the words of a humanitarian prayer from a Unitarian Church service, we may live "so that we may justify our existence in time; and render glory to that which is eternal." I believe, and I think that the overachiever in whatever sphere he exists would agree, that *taking* glory from life is not the only or even the ultimate goal—*contributing* glory is.

What, however, is the value and what are the pitfalls of achievement in its more mundane business sense? Soaring into the philosophical stratosphere may be beyond the expectation of the reader of a business book—although it seems to me that philosophy is appropriate to all practical men. Surely it is one of the talents of the practical businessman, and of the overachiever in particular, that he can translate the principles of achievement from their philosophic to their practical plane.

My fundamental thesis throughout this book has been that *successful business is successful for people.* The most obvious way to prove this, simplistic but persuasive, is to look at the difference between the underdeveloped and the developed nations.

In late 1973 I visited a slum of tar-paper shacks—a slum of the type that tarnishes the outskirts of almost every Latin American city like a spreading human mold—in the town of Cali in Colombia. It was raining and I was forced to wade through a sea of mud in order to visit the tiny shacks in which lived thousands of Colombians. In all that spreading mass of hovels, I saw only one made of good wood and built sturdily with nails. It was small, but no smaller than others, and at least it did not leak in the rain. It had been a shipping case for the furniture imported by one of the wealthy American businessmen who lived down the street.

The general manager of the Colombian Colgate–Palmolive Company, Scott Jefferies, has lived in Cali for almost twenty years and he and his wife have taken upon themselves the task of trying to help the Colombians. They have raised money for a school, provided health aid, talked about birth control, even tried to help the slum dwellers get started in some form of cottage industry. But when all is said and done, it is only those slum dwellers who are able to obtain employment at Colgate or some similar company who can break out of the slums and live decently.

The rescue by industry is the only practical rescue from poverty today. There are many theories of why poverty exists and how it may be eliminated. Libraries of economics and sociology overflow. But the theories of how to reorganize an underdeveloped nation's life are different from the businessman's practical, everyday reality. Even if the theories are valid, the business achiever has to deal with what is real, given, existing. In that context, in today's world, it is very obvious indeed that strengthening business helps people.

What does it mean to "let him be poor"? Shaw asks. And he answers that it means:

Let him be weak. Let him be ignorant. Let him become a nucleus of disease. Let him be a standing exhibition and example of ugliness and dirt. Let him have rickety

*children. Let him be cheap, and drag his fellows down
to his own price by selling himself to do their work. Let
his habitations turn our cities into poisonous congeries
of slums. Let his daughters infect our young men with
the diseases of the streets, and his sons revenge him by
turning the nation's manhood into scrofula, cowardice,
cruelty, hypocrisy, political imbecility, and all the
other fruits of oppression and malnutrition. Let the un-
deserving become still less deserving; and let the deserving lay up for himself, not treasures in heaven, but
horrors in hell upon earth.*

It is instructive to compare this slum in Cali with the worst
slums and the poorest suburbs of large cities of the United States
or England or any other developed country. Admittedly houses
in these areas are small and the apartments terribly over-
crowded; surely dirt and crime abounds; but there is generally
at least a semblance of water and heat; most of the people have
shoes on their feet. Certainly no unskilled laborer living in an
American slum, not even a welfare black in the worst slums of
the American ghettos, would be *proud* to live in a discarded
packing case.

It is wealth, which in today's real world is the result of industry, that creates or allows to exist virtually all of the factors that
constitute "the good life."

Consider health: it is industry, not medicine, that develops the
new drugs to cure our diseases. Consider family size and family
planning: it was industry, not Planned Parenthood, however
worthy that organization may be, that developed birth-control
methods to make family planning practical. Consider education:
it is industry, either directly or through such industrial offshoots
as the Ford Foundation, *et al.,* that funds universities, pays for
modern scholars to do research, and encourages educational
experimentation. At a dinner given for Brandeis University in
mid-1974, the Chancellor said that the vast majority of the dona-
tions he needed each year to maintain and further build that
great university came from business sources. Consider the tech-

nology of our comfortable life: it is the economic motivator that leads to better houses and better cars; it is the economic motivator that reduces the price and improves the ease of travel; I have no doubt that it will be the economic motivator, far more than political leadership or international diplomacy, that will resolve our crisis in energy.

Serious charges are leveled against business and the business community. They are largely myths, but they gather in popularity, especially among the young. (Fortunately, they largely disappear once the young become involved with business and realize that reality is different from myth. Business, the young man finds, may not exist for objectives of specific morality, but it is not immoral; and its driving force turns out to be one of the greatest forces of good.)

The myth of the evils of business can be found in many forms. There is the Marxist myth that industry exploits the worker because it pays him less than he produces: the worker is everywhere in chains, the capitalist everywhere overpaid.

It is true that certain overachievers are paid incredibly well. But this is not primarily payment for their investment; it is payment for their ability to achieve. Who can say in all sincerity that the worker is exploited when it is the activist, the "man who makes things happen," who makes for his standard of living?

Of course, there are industrialists, and perhaps overachieving industrialists, who seek to exploit the worker by paying him too little and working him too hard. But few of these succeed in the modern world for long because the process of competitive business is such that for every exploitative employer, there is another who will take advantage of the exploiter and double his achievement by *not* exploiting the employee!

There is also the myth that industry does not or cannot do anything directly about social ills. David McCall, President of the McCaffrey and McCall Advertising Agency, wrote an article for the May 1973 *Harvard Business Review* called "Profit: Spur for Solving Social Ills," in which he talks of the "grand delusion . . . that the dreadful social problems of the United States—whether racial, environmental, or social—are going to

be solved by the energetic efforts of American businessmen."
He says that this is a delusion because businessmen cannot make
social changes—at least not by trying. But he concludes, in my
opinion correctly, that they should not be asked to do good
(however "good" may be defined) but rather that they should be
asked to make a profit. He explains that if such profit is arranged
so as to be synonymous with good, then good will result. In my
opinion this is close to being the whole point. Business is all
about the achievement of profitable matters. However, those
matters are likely to be profitable only if they are in line with
what people want; and if they are what people want, they are,
in our democratic system, "good" by the only definition applicable.

A third myth is that industry is to blame for a variety of specific
sins:

As noted earlier, false advertising is one of the most often
cited business sins. Largely, the accusation is false. On the other
hand, the benefits conferred by the advertising industry are
rarely mentioned. The accusers do not usually point out that the
industry also makes possible the widest imaginable dissemina-
tion of news, both by making inexpensive television sets available broadly and by financing the news media themselves. In a
paper written for the Aspen Institute for Humanistic Studies
Conference for the Communications Industry in January 1973,
Douglass Cater, Director of the Aspen Program in Communications in Society, wrote that: "Merchandising does determine the
amount of news the citizen receives. Newspaper column inches
rise and fall in approximate ratio to advertising content." Apparently Mr. Cater was concerned about this. But ours is a society
in which the enormous amount of information we receive day in
and day out—and the numberless sources from which we receive it—guarantees more than anything else that we can maintain our press's freedom. The advertising industry, by supporting
the press and television on such a broad economic base, provides us with one of the stronger pillars of our democratic system.

Pollution is said to be a curse industry has brought upon us.

It is forgotten that it was industry that brought us first the good things of life: the automobiles, the appliances, the heated houses that people cried for. It was more people, not more industry, that caused pollution. Industry is merely responsive to public demand; it is not its creator. Now that the public wants antipollution devices, industry is providing them.

The neo-Malthusians scream, as they have always screamed, that the world is coming to an end. The Reverend Malthus predicted starvation for an ever increasing number of people in England. Worse, he implied that there was no hope, that the starving would never rise above starvation. His disciples maintain that pollution will destroy us. The statistics are more sophisticated, but the wail is similar. They too fail to realize the enormous impact that technology through industry can make. Just as Malthus proved to be wrong because technology, hand in hand with industry, solved the problem of insufficient food in England, so his descendants will, I believe, be proven wrong because the same combination will solve the pollution problems of the world.

Inflation is blamed upon industry. The blame is, I believe, unjustified. Milton Friedman and the "monetarist" economists state that only the money supply is able to heat up or slow down the economy. Friedman's theories may not be right, but there is little doubt that in recent years his predictions about recession and inflation have been closer to accuracy than have the predictions of nonmonetarist economists, or indeed of almost anyone else. Moreover, the nonmonetarists include the money supply, along with governmental fiscal policy, such as interest-rate and tax-level setting, as the main forces affecting inflation. Virtually all economists agree that it is not business but government that controls inflation.

Admittedly, I am on tricky ground when I discuss inflation, for no one fully knows the mechanics of what may be a curse or, up to a point, a blessing. No one even knows to what extent inflation is desirable. The stimulation of our economy needed for new technology, new business, new growth, would be insufficient if zero-inflation were the case. On the other hand, we all agree that excessive inflation is unhealthy. However, there is far less doubt that our economic survival does rely upon the increase in the efficiency of production; without that, all inflation would lead to a reduction in the standard of living. It is industry, and industry alone, that can be effective in so improving efficiency.

Finally, there is a new "sin" of industry, namely that it has suddenly—almost maliciously—lost its effectiveness. It is said that industry cannot deal with the energy crisis and that its inefficiency is aggravating the oil shortage. Industry is blamed for not curing unemployment. It is castigated for allowing our cities to die. There is cause to complain. But the validity of the complaints in no way proves that industry is losing its effectiveness.

In the first half of 1974 alone, in response to consumer demand, industry switched with almost miraculous speed and efficiency from large cars to small; introduced a dozen new health cereals; launched successful campaigns to save energy; created an astounding variety of new leisure-time activities, from a Dominican Republic country club to an Amazon River vacation tour; created an improved golf ball, a better fishing rod, an untold number of new fragrances, and a new approach to sun protection. At the world economic level, industry pioneered new economic ties with the USSR, underpinning the rather warm peace that recently has taken the place of the cold war. Industry, represented by David Rockefeller, opened banking connections with Peking, making both news and history. In impressive summary, industry employed countless millions of new additions to the labor force and, in general, continued with "business as usual."

There is no indication that business has lost its effectiveness; if anything, it is becoming more effective.

Which brings us back to the men who create the motive power in business and to the question of where their future lies. Their development, training, and motivation are becoming as important today as has been the education of the ruler throughout history. In many ways they are inheriting the same influence that the rulers of earlier societies wielded.

To fulfill this role, and wield their relatively new and growing power wisely, there will have to be an alteration in the kind of men and women who influence business. The overachiever of the future will be a different sort of man, I suspect, from the overachiever of the past. Not in his motivations, merely in his methods of achieving his objectives.

As businesses grow larger, the new overachiever will have to establish a new kind of openness to ideas. The chief executive officer of a multifaceted conglomerate can no longer afford to brook the sort of attitude which led some early Lever Brothers wag to write across that company's corporate organization chart:

> *Across this tree*
> *From root to crown*
> *Ideas flow up*
> *And vetoes down.*

The overachiever of the future must develop in himself a new wisdom. Theodore Levitt pointed out in 1960 in his famous essay, "Marketing Myopia," that the difference between a "growth industry" and an industry that is not growing is executive perspective and leadership. I would say more specifically that it is the perspective and leadership of the overachiever, for it is the overachiever's leadership that gets results. Levitt gives many examples of how decision makers' narrowness of vision led to the demise of growth industries. I believe that as companies grow into multibillion-dollar corporate empires and controlling them becomes ever more difficult, their leaders will need a greater business vision and wisdom than ever before. This perspective will be needed in disparate ways:

It will be more necessary than ever before for business to choose the right men in order to be able to delegate to them the achievement of the corporate goal. "You will certainly not be able to take the lead in all things yourself, for to one man a God has given deeds of war, and to another the dance, to another the lyre and song, and in another wide-sounding Zeus puts a good mind," wrote Homer in the *Iliad*. In the *Odyssey* and *Iliad* of modern business nothing could be more true.

It will be necessary to avoid acquisition for the sake of acquisition, as has been the case too often in the past. Acquisition can be effective only where it leads to real synergism.

The acquisition by Colgate–Palmolive of the Kendall Company was such a synergistic acquisition: Colgate is particularly strong internationally whereas Kendall was weak. Kendall had major areas for cost reduction, in which Colgate excels. Similarly, Colgate's acquisition of the Helena Rubinstein Company will result in Colgate's expanding successfully into a profitable new business (high fashion cosmetics), and in Helena Rubinstein becoming far more successful through improved administration.

To maintain a balance between profit and public service will be a vital requirement for the new executive. Profit, if not the immediate aim of all business, is certainly its ultimate measure of success. It is almost axiomatic that long-run profitability will be possible only for companies that give consumers what they want. When consumers want business to make an effort to support the common good in addition to providing good products or services, then business and its leaders will have to fulfill this need. In the United States today—and to some extent elsewhere —we appear to be reaching for a new standard of morality and public help. If we are, then business must cater to this new standard if it is to survive. In this context I believe that profits and public service will become increasingly intertwined. The new overachiever will see how to tread a path that accurately encompasses both requirements.

It will be necessary for the new overachiever to develop better measurement devices. When Alfred Sloan was building General Motors he recognized, perhaps more clearly than any other major executive, the importance of measurement:

> *The important thing was that no one knew how much was being contributed—plus or minus—by each division to the common good of the corporation. And since, therefore, no one knew, or could prove, where the effi-*

ciencies or inefficiences lay, there was no objective basis for the allocation of new investment.

The need to develop the best possible measurement devices is far greater now than Sloan could have imagined.

Finally, as business intertwines with society at every level—influencing politics, nations, the whole world; employing every type of person; stretching into every corner of human life—there will have to be a new spirit of compromise. Arthur Waley describes the triumph of Confucianism as "due in large measure to the fact that it contrived to endow compromise with an emotional glamor."

I am convinced that it will be the task of the overachiever in business to make compromise in the business community *emotionally glamorous.* As business grows in complexity and a single corporate religion is no longer feasible, a variety of directions will emerge in major corporations. Each is likely to be sponsored by a great overachiever. If constructive compromise is not possible, anger and antagonism will destroy the corporation. The new overachievers will have to be able to achieve the sort of compromise that accelerates action. Confucius, the Master, said: "The true gentleman is conciliatory, but not accommodating. Common people are accommodating but not conciliatory."

In the future, as today, it will be the overachiever who continues to create the action necessary to move business and thus the world; it will be the overachiever who ultimately moves all those around him. The Master also said: "The essence of the gentleman is that of wind; the essence of small people is that of grass. And when the wind passes over the grass, it cannot choose but bend."

Index